Rock 'n' Rail

A Lifetime Passion for Railways and Rock Music

Richard Clarke

GRESLEY
BOOKS

Rock 'n' Rail

First published in Great Britain in 2024
by Gresley Books
an imprint of Mortons Books Ltd
Media Centre
Morton Way
Horncastle LN9 6JR
www.mortonsbooks.co.uk

ISBN 978 1 85794 601 7

Typeset by Druck Media Pvt. Ltd.

Acknowledgements
Thanks to Janet my wife and those who have helped in refreshing my memory.
These include Adrian Vaughan and Nigel Harris, whose positive feedback helped keep me going with my first manuscript. Thanks also to Rob Crew for not only his drumming but for his enthusiasm regarding the days of steam especially when GM at the Main Line Steam Trust (GC) at Loughborough, when railways were far better.

This work is dedicated to two of my dear friends, Nigel Dalton and Graham Neve, who sadly are no longer with us

Contents

PART ONE

CHAPTER 1

The Formative Years

Nottingham Jubilee 45636 Uganda at speed approaching Trent Junction. (JF Henton)

Mother, or Plum as she was called, due to her shape, had always said it was a train that first made me sit up in my pram. At what age I don't recall. However, the outcome of this event has since played a major role in my life. As a post-war baby and never having known the railways in pre-nationalisation form, the sitting-up in the pram episode must have been motivated courtesy of the London Midland Region of British Railways in West Bridgford, Nottingham.

It is said one remembers little of one's childhood until about the age of three or four and I was no exception. I do however recall my first train set. It was a Hornby clockwork 'O' gauge that I received at the age of five. Years later, Granddad arrived with a box of second-hand model railway equipment acquired at Harry Ingles, a 'junk' shop on Mansfield Road, these being 'OO' gauge and electric. It was far more advanced than the old clockwork 'O' gauge. The seed was sewn! The two pacific locomotives named, *Sir Nigel Gresley* and *Duchess of Atholl*, soon took place of honour within the model layout hastily glued down on father's billiard table. After much remonstrating by father, and numerous threats of

No. 45565 Victoria *heading towards St Pancras at Plumtree. (W Philip Conolly)*

being incarcerated in my room for an undefined length of time, *Sir Nigel* and the *Duchess* won, and father never played billiards again.

My passion for railways grew along with a similar passion for music, especially rock 'n' roll. Bill Haley and the Comets had just released Rock Around The Clock. Such musical excitement! Until the late 1950s we had to suffer a diet of Ruby Murray, Alma Cogan, Max Bygraves, Pat Boone, David Whitfield and Dorothy Squires. We listened on the radio to The Navy Lark, Billy Cotton, Take it From Here and Life With The Lyons. We watched Quatermass, Dixon of Dock Green and Sunday Night at the London Palladium hosted by Tommy Trinder. Conversation seemed to centre around 'did you see so and so on Sunday night at the London Palladium?' or 'wasn't Quatermass exciting?' Soon the quiz and comedy programmes arrived with Criss Cross Quiz, Mike and Bernie Winters, Charlie Drake, David Kossoff and Peggy Mount in The Larkins. Plum modelled herself on Peggy Mount!

The radio gave way to TV, the bland ballads and orchestras gave way to rock, and saddest of all steam gave way to diesel!

The railways started to change and so did the music. Along came Little Richard, Jerry Lee Lewis, Eddie Cochrane, Gene Vincent and a host of artistes from America. How refreshing, how exhilarating. I especially liked the Crickets and Buddy Holly but Cliff and the Shadows were the 'superstars' of the day. The sound of the Shadows was difficult to replicate on my newly acquired Wonder acoustic guitar. I much preferred the sound of the Ventures to that of the Shadows. The Tornadoes were another popular group at the time, although their popularity was short lived, as was the popularity of Adam Faith, Jim Dale and Terry Dean – although Adam Faith's backing group, The Roulettes, were probably far superior musically to most at that time. They later went on to greater things as The Zombies and in the 70s as Argent.

Lonnie Donnegan made some impact during the interim period, from ballad to rock with home made music played on washboards and tea chests called skiffle. This too was short-lived, and not until the early 60s with such groups as the Pretty Things, Screaming Lord Sutch, Downliners Sect, Yardbirds and of course the Mersey Sound did the music scene really take off.

I yearned for a solid electric guitar. Meanwhile I had to make do with electrifying my acoustic guitar. This sadly led to another threat by father to incarcerate me in my bedroom. I was not too conversant with the electrics of father's pride and joy: the highly-polished Fergusson radiogram with its hydraulic lid. I had left my throat microphone, purchased from the army surplus store and fitted to the guitar, connected to the stylus head of the record player, along with its cable. The plug at the guitar end of the cable resembled the mains electric cable for the radiogram. father, returning from work, inadvertently plugged this directly into the mains socket with astonishing results! The hydraulic lid never worked again.

School was tolerated, reluctantly. The teachers were rarely animated or inspirational. Lessons were spent watching the teacher writing copious notes from his book onto the blackboard, while we in turn copied all that was written on the blackboard into our books. A wonderful system of getting information from the teacher's book to our own without passing through the brain of either of us. Consequently, very little information was retained.

Anyway, there were far more exciting things to do with one's time. Collecting railway engine numbers and names, or trainspotting. It was all the rage at the time and I embraced this wholeheartedly. I had

discovered a railway bridge a mile from our house in Bramcote on the stretch of line between Radford Junction and Trowell Junction on the midland line north of Nottingham.

At certain times of the day, to correspond with the passage of the few express trains that used this route, a posse of like-minded trainspotters cycled along the lane leading to the bridge to witness the passage of the 'Waverley' (St Pancras-Edinburgh) and the London-Bradford expresses. Armed with the Ian Allan Combined Volume (the spotters bible) of all locomotive numbers and names on BR we waited in hope for a 'cop' (an engine we had not seen before). After several visits we knew most of the local engines and their names. We would shout obscenities at those that passed regularly. *North Borneo, Jellicoe, Uganda, Hong Kong, Gwalior, Fiji, Ulster.* These were known as Jubilee Class locos and were perhaps one of the nicest proportioned locomotives ever designed. They were also quite common, and along with other designs known as the 'Black 5' hauled the mainstay of express passenger and express freight trains on the Midland main line.

Truancy was rife! This deceit necessitated being able to forge skilfully to convince teachers that one

No. 45520 Llandudno double heading through Oxenholme. A magnificent sight. (John Clarke)

No. 45543 unrebuilt Patriot Home Guard. *She was normally seen every time I went to Derby. (RH Short)*

had not attended school because of some illness or another. I became very proficient at this art and could forge Plum's handwriting undetected. I would probably have made a decent living out of this skill in future years had I pursued that career path, but if any sickness record from my school days had been scrutinised then I would have been unemployable!

It was at my new school that I first met Nigel. Both he and I arrived at the same time and were immediate outcasts as neither of us had the mandatory school uniform. Our respective mothers, in what could only be described as in a manner most 'unfortunate', had dressed us both alike. Grey, short trousered suits in an 'itchy' worsted cloth. This strange apparel was temporary until the school outfitters shop in Nottingham made our uniforms. Mine arrived within a week or two, whereas Nigel's never did. Either by accident or design. He always seemed to be in the grey suit, which I later envied as the correct school uniform was hideous, and no doubt designed by someone with a perverse sense of humour. Green, black and white broad stripes! We were regarded as the sons of gentlefolk by our teachers and parents, and it was of great social standing to be seen as such by those who were aspiring. For those people, this second-rate public

school was considered 'a very proper' school. The fact that one learned very little did not matter, as most of the pupils went into 'father's business'. Nepotism was rife.

Games were compulsory. These were led by a sadistic sports master who took great delight in picking on those pupils who found sport a thorough waste of time and energy. Nigel and I considered all

Ex-LMS Jubilee No 45589 Gwalior *and Black Five bringing back happy memories of footplate rides in the early 60s. (Eric Treacy)*

2P and Jub as per the Waverley as often was the case when observed at Moor Lane. (RW Beaton)

No. 45543 Home Guard at platform 6 Derby having worked a special. (Brian Stephenson)

The new age of music starts – Bill Haley and the Comets took the UK by storm. DA haircuts, full skirts and bobby socks all came to life with Rock Around The Clock high in the charts; the older generation couldn't understand it, but the kids loved it. (Alamy)

sport futile and much preferred to hone our brain cells on railways and their geography. Whereas the sports master preferred the muscle-brained school bully and saw little need for academia. Our school was an ideal breeding ground for the military types encountered later in life. Competition was encouraged whenever possible. There were school 'houses' named after the first four unfortunate pupils who crossed the threshold many years before. And these 'houses' all competed against one another.

The sports teacher, who even to a young boy of tender years appeared to be of limited intellect, was always at loggerheads with the headmaster who was a fellow railway enthusiast. The headmaster was the one redeeming feature at this prison for gentlefolk, where school bullying was rife and never addressed. The two main culprits of this were not the slightest bit interested in railways. Consequently, through their bullying tactics, both Nigel and I were motivated to play truant – so at least some good came of it.

Our truancy was strategically planned with the goal of seeking out locomotives rare to us in Nottingham

and exploring scenic places. The main obstacle to these jolly jaunts was of course finance. This problem was overcome by contributions from parents who gave us money to buy our lunch on schooldays at the Elbow Café on Mansfield Road. School meals being inedible, and no doubt the precursor for today's fast-food outlets and supermarkets. So we kept our lunch money to buy train tickets on truancy days. Instead of the speciality of the house at the Elbow Café (jam roly-poly), we made do with a Kit-Kat bar from the school tuck-shop.

We were all forced to take it in turns to 'man' the school tuck shop, situated next to the urinals, and this arrangement didn't always fit in with our jolly jaunts. However, serving in the tuck shop was perceived as an effective introduction to the world of commerce! Little did the headmaster know that it also served as a successful introduction to the concepts of embezzlement and profiteering, not to mention the black market! The only good that ever came out of the school tuck-shop was when a trolleybus flattened one of the school bullies, complete with contraband, while crossing the

Jubilee 45565 towards the end of its life at Blackpool North. (JS Lever)

road. However, as a mark of respect (enforced by the headmaster) we all had to attend the funeral. I declared there and then that I would not attend any more funerals. Later in life I adopted the same principle for weddings! Although funerals are preferable, as they are shorter than weddings, neither are much fun.

Our truancy jaunts tended to be confined to the local area; Matlock or Bakewell and the Derbyshire Peak district. This usually meant steam-hauled Black 5s and if we were lucky, a Jubilee.

The outings also sometimes involved seeing named expresses at Derby. The 'Palatine' (Manchester-St Pancras) and the 'Devonian' (Paignton-Bradford). Jubilees or Royal Scots on the 'Palatine' and Patriots on the 'Devonian'. Royal Scots and Patriot Class locos were all rare to us in Nottingham but commonplace at Derby. They had magical names and we would spend the evenings underlining these, and their numbers, in our trainspotting books. *The Welch Regiment, Llandudno, Lady Godiva* and *Home Guard*. Plum would busy herself preparing tinned fruit and bread and butter for us on our return, whereas Nigel's mother would offer us coffee and chocolate digestives.

On one outing to Bakewell, we were lucky enough to be invited on to the footplate of a Black 5 for the return trip to Derby. Wow! This new experience was

one we both cherished and one that we wanted to repeat. The smells of steam, the metallic sounds and vibration, and of course the sensation of power and speed. From then on, our truancy days focused very much on getting a footplate run. It was usually down to me to do the asking!

We visited Tamworth on the West Coast main line and gathered in a field with hundreds of other 'spotters' – we ventured to Grantham and marvelled at the Pacific locos – the engine change procedure for both North and Southbound expresses. Nigel always preferred the Eastern Region Gresley and Peppercorn pacifics to those on the Midland. Exciting times, especially considering the alternative of climbing a rope with the sole purpose of touching the ceiling with one's head, or playing rounders in a cold and drafty gymnasium being overseen by the 'sadistic one'. We successfully rode the footplate from Grantham to Nottingham and later to and from Pinxton, and a return trip from Derby Friargate. We thought those days would never end.

The tunnels at either end of Nottingham Victoria station constantly billowed smoke and there was the metallic sound of a 'gong' being struck by the wheels of the engine, announcing to the driver they were approaching the signal controlling the entrance to the station. The driver was often unable to see these

LNER 60028 Walter K. Whigham on the Capitals LTD. This A4 was seen north of Grantham many times while trainspotting with Nigel. (AG Ellis)

signals in the smoke and gloom, and was unaware of the speed or distance travelled after entering the tunnel. It was therefore necessary to have an audible alarm. The sound of a steam locomotive straining to haul heavy freight from a standstill, echoing around the overall roof of the station, and the bark of the exhaust becoming silent once the locomotive's chimney entered the tunnel was all exciting to small child. The green-liveried Southern Region coaches on the cross-country Bournemouth-York express. The station shunting loco, which was usually an ancient tank engine that had seen better days, was commonplace in the 50s and early 60s. Hard to believe nowadays that a main line station once existed there as one wanders through the

depressing shopping centre and car park that has replaced it.

Diesels were starting to make their presence felt under BR's modernisation plan. At that time, we didn't realise how far-reaching this would be. We still made expeditions to seek out steam engines and often this meant trespassing on BR property. This activity was carried out at either Nottingham or Toton loco sheds.

One day at Toton we were approached by a railway official and told we were trespassing and that if we were seen again, we would be punished! It was then decided we should get official permission to visit locomotive sheds from Middle Furlong House in Nottingham. This was the HQ of the Nottingham Division of the London Midland Region. The letter we received in response to our request clearly stated that we would not be granted permission to enter railway locomotive sheds and that if we did so without authority, we could face prosecution!

However, not being put off by this, we continued to trespass in Nottingham and Toton, and every time a railway official stopped us we produced the letter. Strangely enough just the official letter heading was sufficient to let us pass. Not one official actually read its contents! However, one Sunday after visiting Toton with Nigel and his father, his father asked to see our letter of authorisation! Having read the said document he was horrified that he had been a party to our trespassing. He said we should not attempt to do this again. Although, I believe he thought us

No. 45519 Lady Godiva was often seen at Derby on the Devonian. (RW Beaton)

No. 45589 Gwalior complete with Fowler tender. I always thought Fowler tenders looked better than Stanier tenders on Jubilees. (Eric Treacy)

No. 45611 Hong Kong passing West Didsbury on the Palatine from Manchester Central to London St Pancras. (DJ Beaver)

brave and daring as he closed a blind eye to future escapades!

He realised our passion and often took us picnicking alongside the railway line at Ratcliffe Junction just south of Redhill Tunnel. This was a superb place to see all types of trains, many at high speed. There was never a long wait before one came into view and we always had advance warning of their approach due to the close proximity of Ratcliffe Junction signal box and its interesting array of semaphore signals. The monstrosity of Ratcliffe Power Station now occupies the site!

Picnics and trainspotting outings also took place on the East Coast main line at Muskham, north of Grantham. I distinctly remember seeing A4 Gresley pacific *Walter K. Wigham* heading south with a trainload of fish. The speed that it was travelling looked dangerously fast for the short wheelbase vans that bounced along behind, leaving the air full of the smell of fish! The guard must have had to hang on for dear life and no doubt he was given a rather wide berth at King's Cross Goods depot on its arrival there!

The old GN (Great Northern) and GC (Great Central) held a fascination to us. Many a day was spent on the Nottingham Victoria-Derby Friargate line and that from Awsworth Junction to Pinxton. We achieved many footplate rides. Further south we managed a couple of footplate runs on the GC to and from Marylebone. The most memorable being the 4.34pm from Marylebone to Nottingham Victoria on a cold snowy January night. We left Marylebone complete with four non-corridor coaches and a good payload of commuters. With pacific locomotive *Iron*

No. 45667 Jellico *(Nottingham's best Jub) at Derby. (Eric Treacy)*

No. 45552 Silver Jubilee – *the original Jub with silver nameplate and number. (MJ Moores)*

No. 45739 Ulster at Skipton Junction. She was a regular at Moor Lane Bridge on the '10 to sixer'. (S Pearsall)

Duke at the head we made good progress, most of the commuters alighting by the time we reached Aylesbury. This was just as well as we then started to have steaming problems and consequently failed at Brackley! We were by now the only passengers. The guard offered us tea and we waited in the cold for a replacement engine. The night was crisp, the sky clear and the only lights were the stars, three gas lamps on the platform and the oil lamps in the signals. Snow lay on the track and covered the sidings. The glow from the firebox was most inviting while a welcoming fire burned in the waiting room.

Eventually we were rescued and arrived at last in Nottingham Victoria at 1am! The station was full of activity and we saw our first Great Western Hall Class loco waiting to take a parcels train from the north of England on to Swindon. It goes without saying that we had some explaining to do when we got home; our parents would never have believed the school had kept us in detention!

Our less adventurous outings would see us on our cycles at Stanton Gate Station on the Erewash Valley main line. Here we would watch the 'Thames Clyde Express' with a Jubilee at its head. We would stand perilously near to the goods line as freight train after freight train crawled slowly towards Toton marshalling yard

It was here at Stanton Gate that we met a direct descendant of the school bullies, called 'Eppi'. He took great delight in threatening us with a knife and drinking our fruit juice from the water bottles stowed away on our bicycle handlebars. He was totally objectionable. However, after several encounters we concocted a rather strange 'brew' for him, which consisted of ingredients that would never pass muster with today's health and safety legislation. We had great difficulty keeping a straight face as he drank this dubious elixir from our water bottles, seemingly enjoying it! We never saw 'Eppi' again.

Our truancy days usually corresponded with football or cross-country running; both activities considered futile. But sometimes, sadly, we had to show our faces on the football field. The only saving grace was that both these activities took place on Bulwell Common. At one end of the football field was the GC main line, and at the other end the GN Leen Valley line. There was lots of activity and always plenty to see. On one occasion while playing football I scored a goal (the first – and the last!). Unfortunately, this was in the wrong goalmouth. Unbeknown to me they had changed ends while I was watching activities on the GC!

I was usually given the position of left or right back while Nigel was given the job of goalkeeper. These two positions were excellent for us to talk and watch the trains. There was never much football activity from most of the boys. Many were overweight and incapable of rapid movement. Only a couple of the 'brain-deads' wasted their energy in pursuit of a bag of air. Most huffing, puffing and running about with

Silver Jubilee at Cheltenham. (P Paye)

much whistle-blowing came from the 'sadistic one'. The only problem for Nigel and I was that we were eventually placed in different school team houses, thus finding ourselves on opposing sides.

We were both eventually given 'promotion' to house captain. I believe that this was done to motivate us into a world of sport but it failed miserably. After all, who in their right mind would want to be captain of a football team? Even today it is a thankless task. Occasionally, the football field had been 'double-booked' and consequently we were expected to take part in a cross-country run. Cross-country running was another torment but we were compensated by the excellent opportunity to observe the comings and goings of Bulwell Common Station at close quarters. After everyone had set off, Nigel and I would keep well to the back, and when appropriate, disappear on to the platform at Bulwell Common, only to reappear at the end of the group of runners when they returned! It amazed our sadistic sports master how fit we were and that we were never out of breath! But then he hadn't been blessed with a great deal of intelligence – either that, or he didn't want the bother of remonstrating with us! We'll never know.

When inclement weather was with us we were forced to stay in class or go to 'the hut', a damp depressing wooden structure normally used for school assembly. This was the equivalent to a torture chamber. No heat, and pointless competitive games – usually boxing. To stay in the classroom was equally bad as one had to spend an hour or so with 'Swisher'. He was the pervert teacher who took great delight in calling you up to the front of the class and then fondled your buttocks while you stood behind his desk. He taught Latin, a subject none of us thought useful unless you wanted to become a doctor. Swisher resembled Ted Heath, the politician, not the bandleader. Both looked suspect and to this day I still think of him whenever I see Ted Heath.

'Eleven plus' came and went. Thankfully I failed. Deliberately! The thought of going to grammar school and having to stay at school for another year was more than could be tolerated. So at the age of 14 and a half I faked appendicitis and ended up in hospital for its removal. The recuperation period lasted far longer than it should have done and my school days were over. However, not for poor old Nigel who had to endure another bout of further education at the sister school to ours. Thankfully both schools eventually closed, either through lack of funds or by the schools inspectorate. And to those people who say; 'school days are the happiest days of your life' must have led exceedingly dull lives after leaving school!'

CHAPTER 2

A Miserable Alternative

Father was one of those 'self-made' men. In other words, he aspired. He was a post-war entrepreneur born of farming stock in Heckington, Lincolnshire. He diversified from farming, married well, and started to make his mark in ladies' clothing. Not literally I hasten to add, but by acquiring several ladies 'mantles and gowns' shops. Three in total, all of them in Derbyshire with the most successful in Ilkeston. He found a niche market selling exclusive garments in areas where one least thought to find them. It was expected that I should follow in father's footsteps. This idea filled me with horror and disappointed my parents immensely. I found the shop utterly depressing, as I did Ilkeston. His employees appeared 'grey' and subservient. They were ideal for the surroundings they were employed in.

Father gave the impression he was semi-retired and consequently managed to find plenty of time for golf. He was a member of two golf clubs, Beeston Fields and Rushcliffe. Along with fellow members, he took great delight in playing the role of successful businessman. Neither ladies' mantles and gowns nor golf appealed to a 15-year-old trainspotter and aspiring rock star. Neither of my parents approved of my hobbies. Plum's caustic remarks about my

Looking out from the back of a GW auto coach on the Minehead Branch passing Stogumber.

No. 46112 Nottingham Scot (Sherwood Forester) passing Low House Crossing. One of the signal boxes visited during my Settle and Carlisle line visit. (R Leslie)

musical aspirations were usually aided and abetted by the 'Daily' (cleaning woman). The 'Daily' wasn't quite daily; in fact she only used to work Mondays, Wednesdays and Fridays, but father always thought she came every day to clean. Plum pocketed the pay for Tuesdays and Thursdays and used to apply a coating of furniture polish on the front door. Consequently, when father entered the house, the first thing that greeted him was the smell of 'Johnson's wax polish'. He never questioned that the Daily ever might have had a day off! In father's mind she had a 100% attendance record!

Father always kept up an image even when mowing the lawn. He would always be seen wearing a three-piece suit, collar and tie. He was seldom seen wearing anything else. He would wear the suit even on holiday, but did make some concession by omitting the tie. It was during a lawn mowing day, while he was emptying the grass box of the wonderful petrol-driven Atco lawn mower, that disaster struck. This disaster affected me, the lawnmower (which never worked properly afterwards) and the goldfish in the ornamental pool. How was I to know that the lever on the handle would start the wretched thing up heading directly for the pool? The sound of gurgling and the amount of steam and smoke that arose from Atco's innards quickly brought father back from behind the rhododendrons bush. I certainly lost some points that day and father's striped lawn never quite looked the same.

Father returned to Ilkeston once a week to count the weekly takings whenever we went on holiday,

leaving Plum and I to amuse ourselves. Being left to our own devices would generally involve some time spent at the local railway station or going to see a show at the end of the pier. Father only knew two holiday destinations and their respective golf courses, so this meant that I became very conversant with Filey and Skegness stations. Year after year we went to one or the other on holiday accompanied by Uncle Bill and Auntie Iris. Uncle Bill later turned out to be my brother! This was most confusing to me, but in years to come I learnt of father's first marriage, of which the outcome had been Bill. Divorce was a taboo subject among aspiring retailers and golfers, and was certainly never mentioned in front of the children.

After many years of holidaying on the east coast it came as quite a surprise one year to find the 'Jag' heading southwest to Newquay. So instead of seeing Eastern Region locos I was privileged to see Great Western engines, with all their gleaming copper and brass. The summer shows were not any better in Newquay, and the only show I recall was one I saw at Filey, seeing an up-and-coming entertainer called Bruce Forsyth in a sketch involving a telephone box and an imaginary phone call. I didn't dislike Filey and found the railway station with its overall roof and level crossings fascinating.

One year on our Filey holiday we teamed up with a golfing couple, Ernest and Ethel. Father had had business dealings with Ernest. He was a fun character, unlike Ethel who always appeared disagreeable and of indeterminate gender. Ernest always showed interest in me, whereas father showed very little interest, never progressing beyond addressing me as 'Boy'. Presumably he could never remember my name! This holiday was marred however by a huge Great Dane dog with whom I shared the back seat of Ethel's Triumph Mayflower car. Plum and Ethel sat in the front. Plum did not like golf, Ethel or father!

Musically I was coming to terms with three chords on my newly bought Hofner Colorama electric guitar and Truvoice amplifier, much to the disgust of father, who forever tried to play down my musical aspirations with his chums at the golf club.

Jerry and the Phantoms, then the Venoms Rhythm Group kindly let me play rhythm guitar with them, until they were forced to disband. Although I had visions of becoming famous in a pop group, I still wanted to drive trains, which did little in the way of impressing my parents. Nigel too had aspirations to drive trains and he too was little interested in following in the family woodworking machinery and engineering business.

It was decided that we would both apply to become engine cleaners at Nottingham loco shed, assuming progression to fireman and eventually driver. The day arrived when we were invited to attend a medical in Derby with the railway doctor. We received a blue cardboard ticket entitling us to travel free from Nottingham to Derby for this event. At the time we were very much amused by Tony Hancock's sketch 'The Blood-Donor' and we had become quite proficient at mimicking the Scottish doctor. Imagine our surprise when the railway doctor turned out to be a Scotsman resembling the one in Hancock's sketch! We had difficulty keeping a straight face, and on the return journey we mimicked the railway doctor, much to the amusement of other passengers. Our train home was steam-hauled and I recall seeing a Jubilee Class loco *Silver Jubilee* waiting to be scrapped outside Nottingham shed. Little did we realise how far reaching the withdrawal of steam engines would become.

Some weeks later we received our respective results of the medical. Nigel passed and received joining instructions to start as a junior engine cleaner at Nottingham. I however, had a 'failed medical' letter on the grounds of colour blindness along with the usual phrase, wishing me every success in the future! This was not a good day. The news had to be broken to Plum and father. This they took surprisingly well and comments were made about how Nigel's family must be sadly disappointed that he hadn't followed in his father's footsteps, joining the family business.

Envy of Nigel was perhaps my first emotion, but after 'feeling sorry for myself' I began to think positively about a musical career. When I announced my alternative plans, Plum and father rather wished I had passed the medical for railway employment! Neither of my chosen career paths pleased my parents. How could their son who had attended the school for gentlefolk, stoop so low as to choose, in their views, a worthless career path? What would the golfing chums say?

Meanwhile I practiced on the Colorama. Unbeknown to me, father had made arrangements with a fellow golfing chum, Herbert Welch, for me to start work as a junior at Herbert's exclusive

Sherwood Forester again. (RW Beaton)

A Triumph Mayflower just like Ethel Ward's. It would be Plum and Ethel in the front, me and Great Dane in the back (no one was happy except dad, who wasn't there!).

gentlemen's outfitters shop in Nottingham. This was my first experience that the real purpose of the golf club was to network and get favours. Strangely enough this practice still works, and in later years I witnessed far too much of this, playing of golf being secondary to the activities in the clubhouse.

I was none too pleased with this outcome. What a contrast! Nigel in overalls, working with steam engines, while I was dressed up like a 20 guinea 'piss-pot' stuck in the basement of Herbert Welch's, solely in charge of raincoats, hats and Sea Island cotton underwear! On occasions Nigel would appear

at the shop during my lunch hour (30 minutes) and would regale me with tales of Nottingham shed. One day he had been allowed to reverse a Royal Scot Class loco (46112 *Sherwood Forester*) on to the front of a London St Pancras bound express at Nottingham Midland Station. Lucky sod!

I worked with 'Tub' Wilson (number 2 sales) and Mr Sharpe (1st sales). Both took their roles extremely seriously and were ideally suited to their subservient roles. They were always competing to impress Herbert. Mrs Powdrill the cleaner made up the team. She had a good sense of humour, sported

of Nottingham. This old part of Nottingham has all sadly gone, with any remaining factories or warehouses being converted into so-called 'luxury' flats for the 'materialistic upwardly mobile jet-set'.

Val Terry, a theatrical agent who sported jet-black hair and a moustache, and who was probably the first 'test pilot' for Grecian 2000, resided in the same building on Bridlesmith Gate as the seamstress. He was also a ventriloquist and had a 'dummy' that looked just the same as him! Val Terry specialised in acts for working men's clubs and miners' welfares. It was through him I learnt about the club circuit and found out about clubs that booked groups.

The *Nottingham Evening Post* newspaper also listed pubs and social clubs where groups appeared. The most prestigious clubs were the Carousel Club in The Meadows and the Variety Club in Radford. Both had resident groups, with the Reg Guest Trio the most advertised; probably because they were represented by Val Terry! Next generation groups played more exciting venues such as The Boat Club, The Dungeon and The Hippo, leaving the Reg Guest Trio to play their repertoire to an aging population.

Sorties to the seamstress, delivering parcels and alterations for customers always involved a quick look at what was happening at Nottingham Victoria Station. There was invariably some heavy freight train waiting a path or just simmering while replenishing its water, the smell of steam always hanging heavy in the air, trapped by the cavernous overall roof.

Sometimes I had a bona-fide reason for being at Victoria, as some parcels were distributed by BR's parcel service. These parcels were usually being sent back to suit manufacturers in the north of England. I took a long time on these visits to the parcels office. Tub always asked why I took so long doing anything that involved escaping from the basement.

How depressing that basement was, with no natural light just fluorescent tubes. Excitement for me was when Tub or Mr Sharpe rang the bell for assistance. This meant I was needed upstairs to serve a customer or worse still, someone was coming down to the basement for a raincoat, hat or underwear. The latter involved measuring the customer with my 'looped' tape measure. If the garment required was for a singlet (old-fashioned word for vest, which in turn was an old-fashioned word for waistcoat) I took great pleasure in passing the measure over the shoulder, in-between the legs and back through the loop over the shoulder, then pulling tightly, listened for a sharp intake of breath and then read the measurement! All quite simple, but oh how dull working in a clothing outlet (sorry, a Gentlemen's Outfitters).

Trips out on the train became rare as the only available times were Sundays, and Thursday afternoons, half-day closing. Was this all I was ever going to do? Father appeared on several occasions

rolled down stockings and a huge backside. All of which were usually displayed when polishing the steps of the open plan staircase.

Humour was thin on the ground. Tub was not as serious as Mr Sharpe and was at least able to talk about railways. His son was a locomotive fireman at Colwick shed and Tub used to catch the train daily from Bingham to Nottingham Victoria. The tea break at Herbert Welch lasted for 15 minutes and conversation centred around tailoring alterations, which for me involved a visit to the seamstress on Bridlesmith Gate, in the old Lace Market district

An early incarnation of The Crescents – prior to the author joining the group.

at the shop, buying everything he was shown in order to impress on Herbert how well he was doing financially. On these occasions I was invited out of the basement by Herbert to serve father. Mr Sharpe scrupulously checked any sales I made and if I had done something wrong he would give me a rollicking in front of the customer. Hardly motivational. I therefore usually stayed hidden in the basement, spending my time brushing the raincoats. I did once have some excitement when I 'dressed' the display cabinet in the basement with a selection of pullovers from the first-floor territory of Tub. However, Mr Sharpe criticised all this as not being correct, as the basement did not sell pullovers! I should stick to displaying my Sea Island cotton underwear!

The motivational hook in order to make my escape was going to be the Colorama. Although any support from parents or Tub was non-existent.

I had learned several Buddy Holly and Chuck Berry songs and was taking an interest in some of the old blues songs of Muddy Waters and John Lee Hooker. My three chords were working wonders. Same chords, different rhythm, with a few twiddly bits seemed to suffice. Mac, a friend of a girlfriend, played bass guitar and enjoyed much the same music as me. He also lived near a drummer who had been professional with a recording group called the Crescents when he had lived in Liverpool. Mac originated from Liverpool and as the Mersey Sound was just emerging with the Beatles, Gerry and the Pacemakers, The Searchers etc. it was decided to

reform The Crescents (only one original member – but who was to know?). We met, rehearsed our repertoire (badly and not too often), learned to talk with a scouse accent and launched ourselves on an unsuspecting public. Thanks to the agency of the original Crescents, in Liverpool, the work rolled in and I bid farewell to Herbert and his team.

Plum was shocked, father didn't speak for ages, and Nigel couldn't believe that I could play sufficiently well enough to become professional. Perhaps Nigel was right, but we got through. We were a three-piece R & B band. Most other groups were imitating the Beatles (three guitars and drums) or Cliff and the Shadows (singer plus three guitars and drums). The only other three-piece group of any significance at that time was 'The Big Three', also from Liverpool. In Nottingham we only had one three-piece band other than the Reg Guest Trio, and they were hardly into the drugs, sex and rock 'n'roll: the Jaybirds. They were led by an incredible guitarist front man, Alvin Lee.

During this period little was seen of Nigel, as the Crescents were playing many distant venues and working three one-night stands a week. Although we were only a three-piece, we did have a roadie, who was also called Mac. Without him the shows would have been more difficult, although Mac always seemed to disappear shortly after our performance, in search of some willing groupie! Our equipment was quite simple, my Colorama guitar had given way to a Gibson SG, and the Truvoice amplifier traded in against a Vox AC 30. A Rogers drum kit; Framus bass guitar and Vox T60 amplifier completed the equipment. The two Reslo microphones for the vocals were plugged into the Vox AC 30, along with the Gibson. Consequently, the vocals were very muffled and extremely difficult to hear, which is probably just as well, as we could never remember the words and often sang out of key.

But the audiences liked us, I think because we were always 'billed' as a Mersey group and everything we played had that choppy up-beat Mersey sound. We were also a little different in our stage wear, black polo neck shirts, black drainpipe trousers and Cuban-heeled Chelsea boots. We also sported Beatle haircuts, but considerably longer. A far cry from Herbert Welch's days. The Crescents also became involved in promoting concerts, although in those days dances or shows would have been a better description. We hired the Elizabethan Ballroom above the Co-op in Nottingham and once a month put on groups we thought might make us some money. The best earner was Tom Jones and the Squires who we had booked eight weeks before It's Not Unusual entered the charts! He was contracted for a fairly meagre fee. Needless to say, Tom and his entourage were now commanding higher performance fees and were none too happy to appear for what we were offering! We made a few bob that night.

I did meet up with Nigel for the odd holiday during this period. He had seen the writing on the wall at Nottingham shed. Diesels had arrived, steam engines were disappearing and the life, the comrademanship were not the same. He quit BR and reluctantly succumbed to the family engineering business.

Nigel had always been mechanically minded, whereas I was just coming to terms with the propelling pencil. When quite young he had once constructed a motorised go-cart that we tested several times after subsequent modifications in Wollaton Park. During the evenings, when the park was closed to the public and the park keeper had gone home, we would roar around the tracks that circumnavigated the lake. We gained access over the perimeter wall with a self-made pulley system. We managed all this without detection and any confrontation. We had several mishaps and encounters with trees and once managed to avert a near disaster with a deer. We did think of converting the go-cart into a boat, as the lake was underused. However, nothing came of this.

Nigel invested in a 1936 Morris two-seater car that he had purchased for the princely some of £20. The car was in a very poor condition, but Nigel renovated it and it was in this we toured some Somerset branch lines. We enjoyed steam hauled trains on both the Taunton to Barnstaple and Taunton to Minehead lines. We gained access to signal boxes on the Minehead branch and to Dulverton box on the Taunton to Barnstaple branch.

We also witnessed the local freight train at Morebath Junction Halt after exploring some of the Exe Valley Railway to Tiverton. This local freight consisted of a Great Western pannier tank engine and one of those wonderful guards vans with the long terrace like veranda. We drank in the atmosphere of the rural Great Western branch. This was a quintessential branch line with its pagoda roofed buildings, the corrugated iron lamp-sheds, the lower quadrant signals, hanging baskets full of flowers suspended from station awnings, and of course the peace and quiet of the 1960s English countryside. This was long before the onslaught of motorways, juggernauts, and so-called luxury long distance coaches – the latter being a complete contradiction in terms (certainly never luxury in those days, and I remain doubtful if you could ever use luxury and long-distance coach travel in the same breath even nowadays). Today, the Minehead branch is beautifully preserved, while sadly the Barnstaple branch, closed in 1966, has disappeared for good.

Nigel progressed in his sports car days to another 1930s model, this time an MG. Meanwhile, I was learning to drive in the group's Cortina and on occasion father's Wolsley. He had downsized from his two-Jaguar days! Official driving lessons were with BSM (British School of Motoring) accompanied by an overly serious and nervous instructor who took great delight in teaching me how to pass a test: not how to drive! This came after my first accident many years later when my Morris 1000 collided into the rear of a Humber Super Snipe while I was observing a beautiful girl who was walking along the pavement! No damage to the Humber but plenty of damage to the Morris. First learning point when driving: always keep eyes on the road and restrict looking at beautiful girls to the bedroom.

Driving was a necessary evil as girls were discovered, although I much preferred to travel by train and took the opportunity whenever possible, but this did not do a great deal for one's image. Liverpool played an important part in my life and I travelled there quite often. I loved the city. Vibrant, great people with a wonderful sense of humour, and my girlfriend was at Liverpool University. There was still plenty of steam to be seen around the North West. Liverpool Central and Exchange Stations still had steam operated local services. And of course, one must not forget the emerging music scene. In other words: Liverpool had it all!

In the early 60s Liverpool had a direct evening service from Liverpool Central via Manchester and the Woodhead Tunnel to Nottingham Victoria; this was my favourite way of returning home. Steam-hauled on the first and final leg of the journey and an electric loco for the Woodhead section across the Pennines. With a long stopover at Penistone, for engine and train crew changes in the small hours of the morning, this experience could never be repeated. Snow lying on the Pennine hills, wisps of steam drifting across the platforms, coal fires under the water cranes to stop them freezing, condensation running down the waiting room windows all added to an atmosphere directly out of Brief Encounter!

I was often the only person making the journey beyond Manchester, the service being run mainly for the Royal Mail. Certainly, there were more mail vans than coaches. Arrival in Nottingham Victoria was around 1am and it was always a hive of activity with parcels and mail traffic. I recall a southbound fish train and a parcels train from the Western Region. The rare locos hauling these were seldom seen during daylight hours. Nottingham Victoria station took on a totally different character in the wee small hours. The sounds, smells, smoky yellow light, the general activity and hushed reverence about the place, with the scurrying staff going about their duties. All so different from the routine normally witnessed during the day.

Even with the best will in the world, the privately preserved railways of Britain have not yet replicated an atmosphere which comes close to the way things were in the 60s. The closest to the correct ambiance and atmosphere is the Great Central at Loughborough. Much of this, I am sure, is down to Bob Crew its general manager, ex-drummer with The Crescents and ardent enthusiast of steam.

CHAPTER 3

Rock with The Crescents

The drummer and only original member of The Crescents left because of family commitments (jealous wife). Or at least that was the reason given and Bob Crew replaced him. Bob was a most competent musician with a good sense of humour and he loved steam! Musically he put Mac and I to shame. He had played with another Nottingham group called the Wanderers and he also had a van. This was an old Bedford Dormobile with a customized front-end. Because of its domed appearance, Bob had nicknamed it Harold after his father who had a similar domed appearance!

We rehearsed for a day or two and then busked our way through the 'gigs'. The Gibson SG was replaced with a Fender Strat (Stratocaster) and the sound of The Crescents changed. I must say not always for the better, mainly because of its operative, me. I would spend too much time trying out different tones and effects! The Gibson SG had only simple controls. One electric pick-up, tone and volume. Ideal for the lowest common denominator musician. The Strat was a far more complicated affair with tremolo arm, three pick-ups, toggle switch and an even more complicated system for changing strings and fine-tuning. Strange as it was, there were still very few three-piece groups emerging. However, there was still the much-acclaimed trio, the Jaybirds. They were considered the top group in the 60s; we often bumped into them at some greasy spoon all-night café after a gig. They later went on to become Ten Years After.

The Crescents became popular with the so-called Bohemian set who frequented the Nottingham Boat Club. There were three clubs next door to each other, the Boat, Britannia, and the Union. These last two were for those who preferred discos to live music and tended to attract mods and 'teeny-boppers'. The Boat Club was considered to be more for the intellectuals and beatniks and many of the top aspiring groups of that epoch played there; Rob Storm and the Whispers, Bern Elliot and the Fenmen (from Norwich would you believe?) and of course, the Jaybirds.

Other names that spring to mind were Screaming Lord Sutch and the Savages, Freddie 'Fingers' Lee and the Shriekers, Spencer Davis Group and Downliners Sect. What talent. It was a great privilege to play the same venues as these top groups of the day. Another venue frequented by the better-known groups was the Co-op ballroom on George Street, where I first saw the Pretty Things and Carl Wayne and the Cheaters. The Liverpool scene had arrived, and Mersey groups invaded the Nottingham gig scene, including the Boat Club.

Another prestigious venue in Nottingham was The Dungeon on Stamford Street. It was here that The Crescents appeared on the same bill as Lulu and the Lovers. Lulu had just entered the charts with Shout. I believe she was only 14 at the time and had a most unfortunate Glasgow accent, unlike the lady she has become today.

The larger 'Mecca' venues, the Palais and the Sherwood Rooms, still had the resident show bands that played cover versions of the current hit parade. Usually badly! Occasionally the Sherwood Rooms would gamble and promote a well-known group, but this was rare. Two that I do recall were Geno Washington and the Ram Jam Band and Shane Fenton and the Fentones. Shane Fenton eventually reinvented himself as Alvin Stardust. The show bands were in decline, as was Cliff and the Shadows. The music world moved on with the Beatles, the Rolling Stones, The Move, The Pretty Things, The Yardbirds and The Who. Parents hated these groups. The media thrived on them and their wild outrageous behaviour.

The Crescents continued with their brand of R & B, and as the popularity of disco rose, the gigs became fewer. Disc jockeys were cheaper than groups. The Crescents either had to get up to date with Beatles songs, turn into an Irish type show band and play the North East social clubs or disband! During this time my thoughts again turned to railways. Bob and I would talk endlessly about trains. We both had model railways and on occasion we would team up with Nigel and his model railway.

The Crescents took on a more sedentary life, playing residency at local pubs and clubs. There were still the town hall gigs, but these became fewer as discos took over. On one occasion we played three venues in one night! Heanor Town Hall, followed by the Conservative Club (late night drinking club and pick-up joint) on Norfolk Place, Nottingham, which was our Tuesday and Saturday nightclub residency, and then on to an all night 'Hooray-Henry' type party in what was then a select area of Nottingham,

Wollaton. We arrived at a pretentious house called 'The Ponderosa'. This latter gig was all a bit of an orgy. While the Hooray-Henrys were trying to impress each other with golf and business tales upstairs in the lounge, their forsaken wives and girlfriends were having a whale of a time rocking and frolicking with the caterers and the Crescents in the cellar-come-ballroom downstairs! Roadie Mac was supplying all that was needed in the form of TLC!

For some months we existed in semi-limbo until one snowy New Year's Eve after playing at Bourne Corn Exchange Bob managed to tip 'Harold' over on some ice close to Clifton Bridge. The van was a write-off but we still continued to gig. It became very costly hiring transport and shortage of money started to become a problem. Was there any way I could get a job on the railways? When needs must, the devil drives.

Screaming Lord Such in action. Freddie Fingers Lee played piano and lost his eye during Such's horror act.

CHAPTER 4

From Toton Centre Box Lad to Signalman Castle Donington

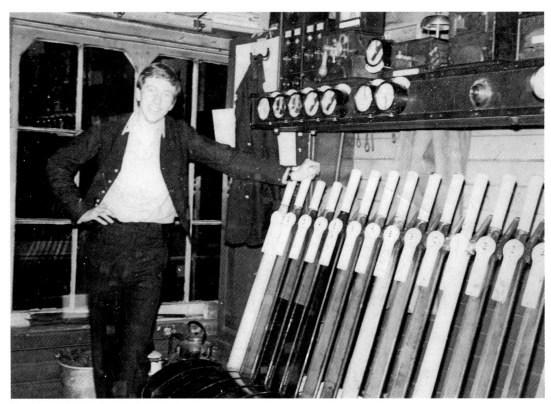

The Author in his first box, Castle Donington.

I applied once again for a job on the railways, this time at Toton. Toton was the largest freight marshalling yard in Britain. But what was I going to be? I didn't really care, provided I was working for BR. Mr Mugglestone, the yardmaster and big white chief at Toton, advertised that there were vacancies, but I needed to pass a medical. Would I still be colour blind? And if so, would this be detected?

Yet again, the blue cardboard ticket arrived and I once more travelled to Derby. Not hauled by a steam engine this time, but in an unfortunate diesel railcar. The faster it went the more it rattled, and the hotter it became. The lights on the return journey also got brighter with increased speed! The same Scottish doctor conducted the medical. Doom and gloom set in on that cold rainy night returning from Derby in that awful diesel. It is strange how one never noticed what a depressing station Derby was when there were steam trains to see. But with the advent of diesels, one was compelled to look around in search of something more pleasant to the eye. Sadly, Derby station did little in this area, and even now it is still a depressing station.

Imagine my surprise when I received through the post my joining instructions. I was to start on BR and should report to the Yardmasters Office at Toton the following Monday at 0900. I had passed my medical! Was I colour blind? Had the original medical report been wrong? We shall never know.

For once, I entered Toton depot officially! It was a bright sunny day and I was there promptly at 0900, courtesy of Plum's bicycle. The admin department was a little hostile, staffed by overweight grumpy women. Thankfully, this was not where I would be working. I was going to be a control reporter at the Centre – whatever that was. I was to receive a basic wage scale of 147… another mystery. Was this £147 per year? Per month? Or what? It subsequently turned out to be 147 shillings per week. Evidently all wages grade salaries were quoted in shillings.

Induction was unheard of. I was measured for a uniform, given a rulebook and escorted by an elderly railwayman, who said he was a 'green-carder', and was taken to the Centre. He puffed and grunted along and told me he was the general messenger and that his duties consisted of delivering mail to all the locations around Toton yard. It was some time later I found out that a green-carder was someone restricted to light duties because of a disability. The name originates from a small green card label that would be displayed on the sole-bar of any defective railway vehicle requiring attention the next time it was to enter the workshops. We crossed many sidings before crossing the main running lines and arriving at the Centre, this being the abbreviation for Toton Centre signal box.

For some reason, I had always thought that signalmen were those unfortunates who had returned from the war disabled. Wrong. On entering Toton Centre I was met by the wonderful aroma of frying bacon and toast plus the sound of signal and point levers crashing and the telegraph bells (block bells) used to communicate between signal boxes. All this was new to me; I had little knowledge of signalling. All I knew was that if the signals were 'up' then there was a possibility of seeing a train. Toton Centre was a complete hive of physical activity and could not have been operated by any disabled returning war veteran.

The operating floor was entered by means of a concrete staircase, Toton Centre being a fairly new signal box constructed in concrete and brick in 1949, replacing an older Midland Railway wooden structure. A young lad of similar age to me was confidently dashing around throwing levers about

and ringing the bells, while an older man was sitting at a long table that was covered by a newspaper tablecloth. He was munching his way through a bacon and egg breakfast.

I was introduced as the new 'box lad' which was the common name for a control reporter. The young lad working the signal box was Alan. He was the control reporter I was to replace as he was soon to be employed, as a signalman, in his own signal box at Attenborough Junction. The man at the table was signalman Eric Elliot, a small hyperactive man with huge bushy eyebrows, a billowing deep voice and wearing 'made to measure', but not for him, railway issue trousers. These he wore at half-mast that appeared to be the result of his exceedingly short bracers! He gave the impression of being worked by a puppeteer though this was somewhat at odds with his deep voice! Evidently it was normal practice for the box lad to operate the box while the signalman ate his breakfast. This of course was unofficial practice – bending the rules. I later learned that if the rules were not bent then 'nowt' would move! Just don't get found out or be seen bending the rules.

My role was to record all the times of the bell signals transmitted to and from the boxes either side of Toton Centre, all train movements and report activities to the Control Centre in Nottingham. I was also to keep the signalman informed of trains due, and which trains were to change engines along with any train crew changes. One had to record all engine numbers too. This was great… I was being paid for trainspotting!

Many through freight trains from the south changed engines or train crews at The Centre, while many freight trains from the north terminated on the New Bank sidings or the Old Bank sidings at the back of the signal box. Trains terminating at these sidings had their train engine detached, which was then forwarded to us for sending it across all the five running lines to the shed for coal, water, turning, if steam, or if a diesel, to a north bound yard or siding for its return working.

This movement of locos changing direction involved many lever movements and much skill in order not to stop the through running of trains on the main lines. There was still a local passenger service along the Erewash Valley and the daily 'Thames Clyde Express'. If you were to delay an express you could expect a 'please explain' letter in the railway post, delivered by the 'green-carder'. If your response was not satisfactory you might then receive a 'Form 1'. This usually ended up with some sort of punishment and was delivered personally by your superior. A suspension or, worse still, removal from your post could follow. Hence there was a great deal of covering-up of any misdemeanours. The railway discipline procedure had been based on Queen Victoria's army!

The New Bank was a modern affair with 'hump' marshalling of inward wagons. Once the train engine had been released, a diesel shunter propelled the wagons over the hump. Once 'over the hump', the wagons would be segregated and would gravitate to either the West or East yard, and were remarshalled for their onward destination. Their speed was regulated by devices that grabbed the wheels, called retarders. These were worked from a control tower directly behind Toton Centre box. This side of Toton was known as the 'Up side'. A similar configuration existed on the 'Down side'. In railway terms it was always 'Up' to London and 'Down' from London. At first this seemed a little odd especially as Toton was very much north of London!

Alan told me he was going to Attenborough Junction once I took charge and he was really looking forward to his first signalling post. He told me Attenborough Junction had a pleasant outlook from the front of the signal box, but the rear was far too close to the local sewage works. This could result in flies the size of donkeys invaded the box during summer!

Engines arriving at the Centre from incoming freight trains often waited a long time for a margin to cross the main running lines. It was difficult to cross them over without delaying a through train on the main line. Tempers were often frayed and drivers became frustrated.

We got to know the drivers who would be in a hurry, and those who would 'slow-time' the movement in order to make some overtime. Drivers from Barrow Hill depot were the worst offenders for slow timing, especially on weekdays and Sundays. With Sundays being paid at overtime rate, it was often difficult to get them to move their engines at all. Barrow Hill men always knew the exact time to arrive at a junction in order to be held up, and consequently, make overtime. However, on Saturdays you would not see them for dust.

One signalman, Bill (tail-lamp) Butler, derived great pleasure from delaying Barrow Hill (men) drivers on Saturdays when they were in a hurry, especially if they had slow-timed during the week and delayed the job (main line running or other movements, or even interrupted Bill's mealtime). He would keenly observe their locomotives' rear tail lamps. If missing, he would have them stopped and thus delay their progress. It was a cardinal sin not to exhibit a tail lamp, thus denoting all was in order and that the train, or engine in this case, was complete. Engines running under their own steam without a train would sometimes not bother to exhibit a tail lamp for the short distance involved between sidings in and around Toton. Bill would gesticulate, shout and swear, and lean out of the window in rage when he saw one of the offending engines. On one occasion, in his excitement, he forgot to open the box window before sticking out his 'red' flag – showering the up goods line in shards of glass and creating a lot of paperwork for himself.

Bill loved to jettison anything unwanted out of the window. On one occasion he tipped the contents of his teapot out of the window on to an unsuspecting guard who had the misfortune to be walking past at that exact moment. The guard was none too happy and stormed up the box steps ready for a fight. Bill told him that it was me who had tipped the teapot contents out of the window! I denied it of course. The guard was told to get out of the box, as only authorised people were allowed entry. He huffed and puffed and used words that would never have been tolerated at the school for the sons of gentlefolk before eventually leaving. In spite of Bill's bluster, we did have some funny moments. On Saturday afternoons and evenings, Toton calmed down and with few train movements Bill would amuse himself by singing rugby songs through the loud hailer system. This system was well amplified and could be heard as far away as Sandiacre; letters of complaint arriving on the desk of the Yardmaster from angry people who lived nearby. Bill received a 'please explain' and vowed revenge on the yardmaster but the songs stopped.

Signalmen worked their three-week cycle in anticlockwise direction. Box lads worked clockwise. Consequently, I regularly worked alongside Bill Butler on afternoon shifts (1400-2200), Eric Elliot on night shift (2200-0600) and Jim Trigger on early shift (0600-1400). I believe I learnt most from Jim; I still practice his advice of 'use your brain to save your legs'.

In signalling terms, it was always necessary that only one train would occupy any one section at a time. Jim referred to this principle as 'one ball, one nut'. On the main running lines and lines used by trains conveying passengers, this system was known as the absolute block system. This applied at Toton Centre on the Up and Down main lines while the goods lines and those only used by trains not conveying passengers were worked under the permissive block system, allowing several trains to follow each other, but only after following trains proceeding into an occupied section were 'cautioned' by the signalman controlling the entrance to the next section.

The three signalmen cycled to and from work in all weathers. Eric from Ilkeston, Jim from Trowell, and Bill having the shortest distance from Sandiacre. I cycled from Bramcote on Plum's cycle, complete with basket. Both signalmen and box lads had one rest day a week. On these days we box lads had to adopt a different way of working. The 'relief' signalmen, who covered for the regular signalmen, often bent the rules and considered his way of doing things far superior to those of the regular signalmen. The relief signalmen encouraged us to do the signalman's job as well as our own, while they talked endlessly on the internal circuit telephone. The telephone system

My first job as box lad at Toton Centre. Signalman Jim Trigger picking a winner on the locker.

was akin to a giant crossed line and several signal boxes could talk simultaneously.

Great debates took place. Relief signalmen were always looking for overtime and would constantly be interested in how many hours everyone else was working! It was said that the ideal relief signalman should have eight children, be in debt and have a miserable wife. Then they would work all duties required of them offered by the signalmen's roster clerk. The relief signalman always encouraged us box lads to go for promotion and suggested which signal boxes had vacancies. The relief signalman was a fountain of knowledge. I was always eager to glean information about the different boxes, never tiring of the endless anecdotes told over a 'brew'. Would it be possible for me to learn all the rules and regulations, pass the exam and have a box of my own?

The signalmen on relief often had nicknames. There was Lord Trent, who was very upper class and both experienced and senior; having worked the entire higher-grade boxes around the Trent area since 'God was a boy'. 'Twink' Burrows, who always wore a separate collared red and black striped shirt and resembled Jimmy Edwards calling everyone 'Surry'. We also had box lad rest day reliefs. Two

that spring to mind were 'Pinkie Salmon' and John 'Charlie' Chester. Pinkie's father, Stan, was one of the three head shunters in the Old Bank Sidings. The head shunter on my own shift was Herbert and he was an exact replica of Stanley Holloway. Another character employed in the Old Bank was 'Tutty' who was very large and round, the same width as he was high. Tutty had a crane for transshipping displaced wagonloads from 'cripples' (defective wagons). His responsibility on one occasion was to free two 'buffer-locked' vehicles on a car carrying train that had become buffer-locked on the severe mining subsidence undulations on the Erewash north of Ilkeston. The crane was used to lift the wagon directly from behind Jubilee locomotive *Newfoundland* that was in charge of the train. I spent some time 'gawping' out the window at one of the last Jubilees still in active service.

Box lads Pinkie Salmon and John 'Charlie' Chester were based at Trent and Ilkeston respectively. The boxes they covered were other high graded boxes where the traffic density necessitated a helping hand in the way of a control reporter. Box lads also conversed endlessly on the phone, seeking out information as to how trains were running, especially express freight and passengers. Advance information on train running was imperative if the signalman was not to impede the progress of a fast-running service.

There were only two regular steam-hauled fast freights; all the others were diesels. These both ran on the night shift, and it always made night turn that little bit more exiting. These were the Hull-Birmingham and the Lawley Street-Normanton. There were some other steam workings during the other two shifts but these were slow heavy freight trains. Steam was disappearing very fast indeed, while new soulless diesels were arriving at an alarming speed. The sole steam-hauled passenger train was a Sheffield-Nottingham local at 7.30 on early turn, although this only seemed to happen if there was no diesel railcar available. I did manage to see both 45573 *Newfoundland* and 45675 *Hardy* on this service. However, it soon succumbed to a diesel railcar every day.

Clay Cross North Junction, Pye Bridge Junction, Ilkeston Junction and Trent Station South Junction all had box lads. Trent Station North Junction had the luxury of a train regulator who was in constant contact with most of the regulating boxes, with the sole purpose of minimizing delay and prioritizing running.

With the demise of traffic on the Great Central and Great Northern lines through Nottingham Victoria, now transferred to the Midland Region from what was then the Eastern Region, many boxes on these former Eastern Region lines saw little traffic. They retained their classification due to an old agreement with the train unions. Many of the signalmen from the GC were now finding redeployment on the Midland main line, which many found hard to adapt to. The Midland was far busier than the old GN and GC signalmen always seemed slower and less motivated. However, they received payments for travelling from their old location on the GC to somewhere on the Midland.

I learned the job. Alan went off to Attenborough Junction and the world was good. The Crescents performed whenever possible, which often necessitated me changing shifts or having a day's holiday. Nigel visited the Centre on occasion and was sometimes accompanied by his father. My father also visited the Centre even though it was not the place for him to be seen by his golfing chums from Beeston Fields Golf Club. His first remark on seeing lines of rusty 16-ton mineral wagons as he passed the New Bank Yard was 'why doesn't someone paint them?'

Fortunately, his visit did not correspond with Bill Butler's shift. Bill's amplified rugby songs would not have been well received. He did however meet Jim Trigger. 'A perfect gentleman', he said later, while describing his visit to Plum. This was now the turning

The violent criminal Frank 'Mad Axeman' Mitchell never came to Castle Donington Signal Box, even though I expected him to arrive anytime during my first night on my own in the box.

point for Plum, who, up until then had ridiculed all I had done. "How nice for Richard to have a proper job he likes," she told the 'Daily'. This sea change saw her buying me a second-hand Morris 1000 to go to the Centre in. I must have been the only box lad to turn up in a car!

Every two weeks we received 'The Vacancy List'. This was often known as the escape list and I digested it thoroughly; pondering which signal box I should apply for. I read over and over the rules and regulations necessary for one to become a signalman. I applied for all the lower grade signalling vacancies.

Jim Barnes (Gentleman Jim) the signalling inspector and his assistant Cedric Pearson (ex-GN) were like Mr Nice and Mr Nasty. They resembled police detectives in their dark blue rubberized trench coats and trilby hats. Mr Nice would help you with your answers to difficult questions while Mr Nasty wouldn't. I was considered suitable for the post of signalman at Castle Donington. Both Jim and Cedric together at their office on the platform at Trent Station gave me a thorough 'drilling' on rules and regulations. They thought me fit to see 'the chief', Mr McAvoy, and Mr Forester-Fielding the divisional manager at Furlong House Nottingham. This was arranged, and although extremely nervous I was pronounced suitable to the post of signalman at Castle Donington.

The day arrived when I had to report for training at Castle Donington. I was booked to train on middle shift, office hours of 9-5. I duly arrived at 0900, complete with my mandatory peanut butter sandwiches, which I once made the mistake of telling Plum how much I liked when I started at Toton Centre. Every day since I got peanut butter! Even the sparrows wouldn't eat the stuff after the first week at Toton.

Maurice was on 6-2 duty that November morning when I arrived in the goods yard at Castle Donington. The airport was a long way off being built and the station epitomized the quintessential English village station, complete with goods yard. This consisted of three sidings mainly used for the unloading of coal for the local coal merchants. Roy, a goods clerk come shunter, was stationed in the old station booking office and was in sole charge of the three sidings, and the once-a-day freight that shunted the yard. The CEGB (Central Electricity Generating Board) operated the coal-fired power station a mile down the line, where there was still an industrial steam engine for the internal shunting of wagons.

Castle Donington signal box was a beautiful example of Midland railway architecture, having changed little since it was built around the turn of the century. It was kitted out with a black lead stove with top oven, oil lamps, and a chemical toilet! Maurice had been signalman there all his working life. He cooked his bacon and egg breakfast, which floated in an inch of congealed fat on top of the stove.

This cooking process was in an old church collection plate! It smelt wonderful, but looked dreadful. He welcomed me, made me feel at home and explained the working of the box. At 1400 Maurice cycled home to his house in the village of Lockington and Bert replaced him. Bert was a humourless Welshman and I was pleased when he said you might as well go home now. "Make the most of any time you can fiddle while you're training; you won't be able to when you have taken charge."

A Trent relief signalman who had several nicknames was covering the night shift; 'Nan Cox', 'Poisoned Dwarf' and 'Ron the Con'. His real name was Ron Cox and I didn't meet him until the following week when he was on afternoon shift (2-10). He had a striking resemblance to Charlie Drake.

Castle Donington was a very cozy signal box. Its block signalling instruments were highly polished along with the black lead stove and the oil lamp. The latter had to be replenished with paraffin on night shift, usually about 2am. The early turn (6-2) signalman was responsible for bringing coal up, replenishing the paraffin in the oil hand lamp and the light. He was also responsible for all other 'Mary-Anning' (cleaning). This meant washing the floor (Saturday mornings), while window cleaning took place on Saturday afternoons and emptying and replenishing the chemical (Elson) toilet. This last task involved digging a hole in order that the contents of the bucket could be emptied into the hole and then covered up again. Lastly, the bucket was replenished with the correct ratio of chemical fluid and water. This latter task I never quite perfected. No problem with digging the hole or emptying the bucket; my problem was getting the chemical fluid mixture correct. My first attempt after taking charge left Bert in some discomfort after I had forgotten to add the water to the chemical fluid. He eventually went off long-term sick, which then left a vacancy to cover and resulted in much overtime.

It was customary to train a week on all three shifts before being 'passed out' by Jim or Cedric. During the first two weeks I trained with Maurice and Ron. Ron was a larger-than-life character who travelled all over the world, photographing steam, especially industrial and narrow gauge railways. When most railway men had rest days either side of the weekend and achieved little more than shopping or gardening, Ron would have been to northern France, seeking out steam! He sported brown corduroy trousers that hung down to his knees, had a continual snuffle, and had an enthusiastic manner that without fail would carry you along into his world of steam. I warmed instantly to him and we became good friends. We later spent much time searching out narrow gauge industrial steam in France, along with main line steam. France still had steam trains performing duties they had been designed for, on both suburban and main lines.

The third week at Castle Donington I trained on nights (10-6). Night shift in a signal box takes on a certain magical charm. Sounds of wildlife, the stillness, and the nocturnal visit from the local constabulary in search of warmth and coffee. There's just the dim glow from the oil lit signals outside the box and the soft light inside from the paraffin oil lamp suspended over the desk. You are at one with your own thoughts; the fire crackling, a feeling of total contentment. Just when you are starting to doze, the sound of the block bell alerts you. On this occasion the adjoining box, Lock Lane, was offering an express freight train. This was the first time I saw steam at Castle Donington. It was shortly after 2am when in the distance I heard a hard-working steam engine and saw the night sky light up with sparks from the chimney and the firebox glow. It was my old friend from Toton days, the Hull to Birmingham, hauled by one of the remaining Eastern Class B1s located at Hull. No sooner had its rhythmic chuffing disappeared towards Weston on Trent, than Chellaston offered us another old Toton friend in the opposite direction, the Lawley Street-Normanton and yet another steamer! This time it was a Black 5. It limped past, steaming badly and took a considerable time to clear Lock Lane, presumably having difficulty climbing the gradient with its heavy train of steel. These were the only two trains rostered for steam. But they always made the night shift something to look forward to.

I was eventually passed out as competent by Jim Barnes, and took charge on nights just after Christmas. My nervousness was made worse by Plum, who had just heard on the television news that Frank Mitchell the 'axe man murderer' had escaped from Leicester prison. Everyone should be alert to this dangerous convict, the newscaster had said. "Don't forget to lock your door," said Plum on my departure. I was convinced he would find his way to my signal box. I took over from Ron, who after exchanging pleasantries left on his pop-pop (moped). I was on my own. No one to ask what should I do. Could I remember the emergency bell code signals? And more importantly could I remember what to do?

I knew that one day I would have to act, but never realised it was to be the Lawley Street-Normanton that would test my metal on my first night in charge. At 2am I received the bell signal 5-5 (train divided) from Chellaston Junction. The Lawley Street-Normanton had passed Chellaston in two or more portions. I remembered to wave my hand-lamp slowly from side to side to the driver of the 8F as the train approached, to indicate what had happened. Lo and behold, he stopped immediately, whereas he should have continued reducing speed so as to lessen any impact that might happen from the rear portion of his train catching up with him. It appeared that just the guards van had become uncoupled approaching Chellaston. The next train then propelled the guards van forward to Castle Donington to rejoin its train.

Meanwhile, the 8F simmered gently outside while the crew made tea and filled the coalbunker with coal from the engine's tender. Eventually, the guards van and its occupant were reunited with driver and fireman and all was well. It was decided to say nothing, as reporting the incident would mean lots of paperwork. A little altering of the train register book at Chellaston and Castle Donington ensured that the event had never happened.

It was at 4am, shortly after the excitement of the Lawley Street-Normanton that there was a terrible crunching and scraping sound outside the box. The hair on the back of my neck stood up when footsteps came clomping up the box steps. Is this Frank Mitchell? No, it was the village constable arriving for his coffee. Evidently, he had no lights on his cycle and his brakes were none too good either. He had crashed into a newly deposited coal heap in the goods yard. He was not very happy but coffee with a tot of whisky soon perked him up.

My baptism was over and I was very content with my lot. The Crescents disbanded. Bob went to work at his father's print works in Nottingham, while Mac joined the pop group Sons and Lovers. Nigel visited Castle Donington when I was on nights, to witness the passing of the Hull-Birmingham and the Lawley Street-Normanton. These two trains remained steam-hauled throughout my days at Castle Donington. Sometimes a Birkenhead-Stanton Gate was routed via Castle Donington, and this too was steam-hauled. Everything else that passed was diesel hauled. Most of the traffic consisted of coal from Toton to Wichnor, Repton & Willington and Castle Donington power stations. It was always difficult to regulate these freights through the Trent area and they often had to wait for a path for long periods to join the main line at Sheet Stores Junction beyond Lock Lane. Things moved slower in those days. Many were the times that the triangular configuration around Trent got so snarled up with long empty coal trains, that a state of 'checkmate' ensued! It was down to the signalmen to keep this to a minimum. Bending the rules became the norm.

Diversions from the West of England main line occasionally brought a few faster trains. The Newcastle-Bristol mail and sleeper train was quite often diverted via the 'Donington Branch' because of engineering work between Derby and Burton on Trent, otherwise the only other fast movement was the Nottingham-Bristol express freight that came past Castle Donington around 8pm. By strange coincidence this train managed to derail itself twice while I was at Castle Donington. On both occasions at the same spot, and much to the delight of the local inhabitants, shedding its cargo of Raleigh

Nottingham Victoria Station as it often was, especially at night, quiet.

cycles and Player's tobacco over the adjoining field and lane. Fortunately, I was not on duty on either of these occasions – although I was involved with the consequent disruptions to traffic and of course the clear-up operations with the BDVs (break down vans). Another coincidence was that on both of these derailments it was the same Class 45 diesel and driver in charge. The enquiry found that the cause of the derailment was excessive speed.

Mel, the local policeman rostered on the same shift pattern as me, paid regular visits for his coffee. In days of little crime and very little supervision by the police sergeant, the 'bobby' on the beat used a pushbike and made hourly rendezvous at prescribed telephone boxes, where on occasion, the sergeant might appear or he would telephone.

One night Mel arrived in the signal box dropkicking his helmet across the box and clean out of the open window, just as an empty coal train was passing. His helmet landed in the third wagon behind the engine! It was now down to the signalman at Lock Lane to retrieve the said helmet and return it with the driver of a train heading our way. Mel would have had to pay a fiver out of his own pocket if he didn't get it back. An episode followed which took a great deal of explaining: the box window was smashed when the overzealous driver hurled Mel's helmet from the cab of his Class 45 while passing the box at speed.

Every Thursday the AM (Area Manager) stationed at Repton and Willington appeared with the wages. These arrived mid-morning and had to be signed for by the early turn signalman. The wages were for all the staff based at Castle Donington, of which there were 10 (six p-way, three signalmen, and Roy the shunter). The p-way (permanent way) staff were located in the old station buildings along with Roy. These buildings still functioned in spite of the station having closed to passenger traffic some time between the first and second world wars.

The AM made this weekly outing by taxi and must have had responsibility for a considerable amount of money. All staff under the employ of the AM were paid in this manner. The practice continued into the1980s and in addition to delivering pay, special operating notices were delivered along with the vacancy list. The vacancy list always appealed to me and I used to give it considerable thought. I was eager to gain promotion in the signalling grade. Castle Donington was a Class 4 box and was the bottom grade. Consequently, I applied for all Class 3 box vacancies that appeared on the list. This list covered all wages grade vacancies on the LMR (London Midland Region), with the exception of some supervisory grade vacancies. I applied for the Class 3 signalmen's post at Long Eaton Station and subsequently got it.

CHAPTER 5

Long Eaton Station Signal Box

I was sad to leave Castle Donington. It was rustic, from an age past, not rushed, and no problems with delays to fast freights, express and local passenger trains. Whereas Long Eaton Station had all the problems of a main line, plus road traffic, it being right in the centre of the town. It still had a passenger service that ran along the Erewash Valley between Nottingham Midland and Sheffield Midland, operated by unfortunate DMUs (diesel multiple units). This service was little used by the local inhabitants as they were constantly being indoctrinated into the world of road transport i.e. the new M1 motorway.

Marples Ridgeway Construction had helped build this monstrosity and the said Ernest Marples became Minister of Transport. Richard Beeching had been appointed to review the rail system of Great Britain, with a view to downsizing and consequently wielded his axe. Barbara Castle, who later became Transport Minister (known as 'the cow in labour'), was implementing the Beeching Report, with mass closures of the rail network and acute rationalisation. Even the last main line to London, the Great Central from Manchester via Nottingham Victoria to London Marylebone, was to be closed. This had been built to continental gauge with a view to running under the English Channel at some later date, thus it was compatible with most of the rail network in Europe.

There were also only two level crossings between Manchester and London Marylebone, at Torside on the Manchester side of the famed Woodhead Tunnel, and at Beighton on the Sheffield side of the Woodhead. This compared well with many other routes that sported many level crossings. Not only was the GC a fast and modern route it was also electrified between Manchester and Sheffield. Such was the folly of Beeching and the corrupt association between the Government and the road

Hardy, pictured well away from Long Eaton where I rode the footplate to Toton and suffered burnt offerings from Plum for being late home. (John Clarke)

hauliers, at the expense of the general public that the Government was supposed to represent.

If Beeching needed to close any direct route from the north, surely the Midland route should have been the first choice. Either Beeching had no idea of the

The M1 that brought disaster to rail travel. (Alamy)

geography of the rail network or he was in the pay of the road builders. Whichever, he had been promoted way above his intelligence and had no idea of the potential of the GC. Today his actions would have been akin to those of a 'war criminal!' We must think ourselves grateful that he was never appointed as prime minister. The dreadful lack of investment in 50s and 60s has helped make the railways of 21st century Britain the laughing stock of modern Europe.

'Glacier Mint', or George Fox to give him his real name, was my tutor and signalman at Long Eaton Box. George had been signalman at Long Eaton for most of his signalling career and appeared to know everyone in the town. He would continually be waving at someone or another whenever they walked across the level crossing, especially young females! He would give priority to road vehicles and pedestrians alike at the expense to rail traffic. Consequently, he was liked by all the townsfolk and detested by engine drivers. Often a train would be approaching the signal protecting the level crossing gates at a snail's pace while George very slowly wound the gates to close off the road! Train drivers knew when George was on duty, as they never got a clear run through Long Eaton.

Two porters operated the station on a two-shift rota. Early and late turns. The keys to the station and booking office were kept in the signal box. Both porters spent more time drinking tea or coffee in the box than in or about the station. Other pastimes were a swift pint in the Victoria pub adjacent to the station. Railway men love beer; unlike today's railways where all forms of alcohol are forbidden, the railways of the 60s thrived on tea and beer. Strangely enough, most of the managers at that time turned a blind eye or indulged themselves. Long Eaton box was like the Windmill Club – it never closed. It was open continuously with the exception of Christmas day.

Overtime was rife. There was always plenty for both the regular signalman and the relief signalman, George never refusing the chance to earn a few extra bob. When he was not in the box, he could be seen cycling around Long Eaton and Sawley. Like most signalmen, he was proficient in cooking on the stove. He also disliked interruptions at meal times whether by the porters or a train. He was a 'dab hand' at slow timing train movements when he was either cooking his breakfast or eating it. He was also an ardent fan of the Reg Guest Trio, who were still performing.

I was 'passed out' after three weeks' training and took charge on night shift. My old friends, Hull-Birmingham and the Lawley Street-Normanton still passed and were still steam-hauled. Some other old friends from the Toton Centre days were booked through Long Eaton as opposed to taking the high-level route avoiding Trent Station and all its conflicting junctions.

On one occasion we wrongly routed the Stirling to Dover sleeper and motor-rail service towards Nottingham and consequently, cleared signals for the Nottingham direction. The driver, evidently not realising he was routed wrongly until the last moment, made a full brake application. This resulted in several sleeping car passengers falling from their bunks! I personally witnessed the window blinds shoot up in a carriage directly opposite me, which revealed an elderly gentleman complete with 'Wee Willie Winkie' night shirt and hat, looking rather nonplussed, picking himself up from the floor. As usual, nothing was reported.

By late 1966 there was little steam left on BR. The daytime exceptions were the Birkenhead-Stanton Gate hauled by a 9F, which usually returned to Stoke-on-Trent, and sometimes a steam engine from Toton to turn. Jubilee Class 45675 *Hardy* arrived on the Up main line one lunchtime and was sent to Trent Junction to turn for its return working north. It was in a very sorry state. Covered in filth, minus smoke box number plate and nameplate.

It had a diagonal yellow band on the cab side denoting that it should not venture under the newly electrified overhead lines south of Crewe. The driver said that it should never have ventured out at all. It so happened that it arrived back at Long Eaton after being turned at 1400hrs just as Glacier Mint put his cycle under the box. No sooner had he taken charge and I was up on the footplate of *Hardy*, for a trip to Toton North Yard. A wonderful experience, but a long walk back to my car at Long Eaton. Plum's burnt offerings followed when I got home, although her burnt offerings varied little from her normal culinary offerings, haut cuisine having completely missed her generation!

Nigel still turned up to witness the passage of the steam-hauled night freights. One Saturday morning he arrived with his father a few moments before the ex-Station Master (SM) from Trent arrived. The SM was an odious person who lived in a railway house adjoining Trent station. He had become the SM through default or seniority; seniority taking priority over suitability; either that or he had been the only applicant. He was overly pompous, totally rules and regulations orientated and he managed by threat and dread.

His position as SM had become redundant with the arrival of a new breed of area manager and he was now passing his time in the role of inspector, although no one quite knew what his role was other than making minor issues into dramas. He had little purpose under the new regime but was kept in employ until his retirement. This was presumably a cheaper option than paying redundancy. Much dead wood was moved around the network under 'UBA' (Used to Best Availability). All detested him. He ejected Nigel and his father from the box and I subsequently received a severe reprimand for

allowing unauthorised persons into the signal box. Nigel's father, a kind and personable individual, couldn't understand how anyone could make such a fuss over nothing.

In the SM's day, recruitment was completely different. If you could stand up and breathe or were the son of a railway man, you got the job. This presumably is how he got his position. No psychometric tests in those days!

Although he was always on the prowl, this did not deter me or other signalmen from having unauthorised persons visiting. Inspectors and managers alike never seemed to mind the local constabulary visits, however this man had a personal vendetta against everyone, so, whenever the alert was given by means of the 2 pause 2 bell signal on the block bell by the next signal box, any visitors were asked to scarper immediately.

As his only route from his house was over the level crossing at Long Eaton Junction, it was the responsibility of the signalman there to 'sound the alert'. All went well until one day the SM changed his car. He managed to cross over the level crossing undetected and found the signalman at North Erewash Junction in an amorous position with his girlfriend! Females were taboo in signal boxes, especially one female in particular – the SM's daughter! On one occasion the signalman at Long Eaton Junction quickly suspended the said daughter out the rear of the box, just in time, as 'himself' came up the box steps. Without this quick thinking, heaven only knows what would have happened. Thankfully nothing did happen. The SM was none the wiser and his daughter kept her reputation, or at least with her father!

Out of hours visits were frequent and he was known to snoop along the line at night, without a lamp to avoid detection, hoping to catch someone out. However, this practice stopped after he tripped over a signal wire and fell on his face. Creeping around at night often put any inspector or manager in an embarrassing position. There was always something going on that shouldn't have been: in the pub instead of being in the box, asleep on duty, working slack and not using the signalling equipment but describing trains in a chatty fashion over the telephone, unauthorised persons sitting in the box (usually girls), or listening to the radio. Radio Caroline and Radio Luxemburg being popular on nights. Kid Jenson, the Irish Hospital Sweepstakes, Horace Batchelor from Keynsham, (spelt 'KEYNSHAM') were all the vogue then. Tony Brandon, Simon Dee, Dave Lee Travis, Pete Murray, Simon Bates, Jimmy Young, Jimmy Savile and Tony Blackburn were all the signalmen's friends. Procol Harum's Whiter Shade of Pale was played endlessly.

Ron Cox came to learn Long Eaton Station box while I was there. Relief signalmen, if not rostered to cover a signalman's day off, were usually rostered 'spare'. This meant that they should not incur any overtime and that they should either refresh their box knowledge or learn new boxes. Because Nigel also got to know Ron this increased his unofficial box visits to those where Ron was rostered. In fact, Nigel was becoming quite proficient in the art of signalling. He was extremely eager to clear the signals, and sometimes too eager to put them back to danger with sometimes startling results. Drivers never liked to see a signal reversed to danger in front of them!

Another visitor was 'Pinkie' Salmon, who, by now had progressed to signalman Class 3 at Hathern signal box, near Loughborough. Pinkie's turn of duty at Hathern followed mine at Long Eaton, so when I was on 2-10 I would often drive over to see him for a coffee and join him for an hour or two on nights. Likewise, he would often turn up at Long Eaton Station with a bag of chips in the evening before he started his night shift at Hathern. Chinese takeaways were a marvellous invention for us signalmen. Often was the time we would pick up a takeaway en route to work.

It wasn't long before both Mac and Bob, fellow members of the Crescents, visited me at Long Eaton. Bob was already a 'chuffer nutter' and enthused immensely about signalling. Mac too became impressed and consequently they both decided to become signalmen. Both were accepted and I received £5 for each of them as my reward for helping to recruit two signalmen. In those days there was a great shortage of signalmen.

Mac went to learn Attenborough Junction, following in the footsteps of Alan Bullimore who was now to train Bob at Trent Junction. These were both hard worked Class 3 boxes. Trent Junction especially. It was strange that Alan Bullimore, who trained me to be a box lad back at Toton Centre was now training Bob to be a signalman, at Trent Junction. Bob and Mac 'passed out' and we often visited each other's boxes. We could all work each other's boxes... unofficially! Nigel too increased his box visits and the SM never found out.

A new breed of manager started to arrive, called movements inspectors. These were essentially operating people, connected with the day-to-day running of the railway. The area manager was now taking on a more personnel and commercial role, leaving the operating side to so-called specialists. It was always the joke that movement inspectors inspected anything that moved! These inspectors left a lot to be desired. Many had been recruited directly from university and were clueless about railway operations, with little understanding of anything in an adult world.

After obtaining a degree in 'basket weaving' they went on to a management-training course, where they were taught to sit the right way round

on the toilet. Head up! After this initial training they were appointed to their first management or supervisory post. Thankfully, never staying too long. Engineering 'cock-ups' were rife and the signalman had to get them out of many a scrape. They were mostly nice but dim. Because they were unpopular with 'time served' railway managers, they were encouraged to apply for promotion on another area, being given glowing reports in the process. This practice continued for many years and we can now understand how some of the current privatised railway systems have become so badly run.

Mel, my policeman friend from Castle Donington, had now turned up at Long Eaton. He spent many an hour resting in the chair next to the fire between making hurried sorties to some phone box, with the aim of a rendezvous with his sergeant. This he often did using my car! One Christmas Eve he arrived soaked to the skin, his huge cape dripping all over the recently polished floor. From under the cape he produced a bottle of whisky and a turkey as a thank you for all the cups of coffee and the use of the Morris 1000. We drank some of the whisky and I took the turkey home to Plum.

The weekly vacancy list now showed many signalling vacancies, mostly Class 3 and Class 4 boxes. The next steps up the promotional ladder, Class 2, were thin on the ground. However, eager to get a Class 2 appointment I applied for any that appeared. The 'standstill' agreement, negotiated by the trade unions, still existed. This related to a classification once given that could not be reduced. Some Class 2 vacancies appeared along the old GC and GN lines radiating around Nottingham Victoria. These two once principal lines were now a target of the 'Beeching Axe'. Rumours were rife and traffic much reduced, especially on the GN between Nottingham Victoria and Derby Friargate. Many boxes had closed or had reduced opening hours.

The Awsworth Junction to Pinxton branch had closed in 1963 along with all the boxes, and the Nottingham Victoria to Derby Friargate passenger service finished the following year in September 1964, although the line still remained open for freight, and thus retaining some of the boxes.

I applied for Nottingham Goods South box situated on the GC south of the Trent River Bridge, which controlled the junction to Queens Walk goods yard. This box was open solely for the Marylebone-Nottingham newspaper train that arrived at 4am. This would have been an easy Class 2 box, but with little chance of overtime. I subsequently applied for Kimberley on the GN Nottingham Victoria-Derby Friargate line, seeing that this would be a more lucrative Class 2.

I received my allocation to the post of signalman at Kimberley GN (Class 2) and duly started on the same day that steam finished at Annesley and Colwick.

CHAPTER 6

Kimberley Station
East GN Signal Box

Kimberley was a complete culture shock after Long Eaton. The sudden transition from constant activity to complete inertia was something I would have to get used to. It seemed strange that promotion brought less work with far fewer trains. The inactivity was reflected in the lethargy of the signalmen. Serious and sombre would best describe their demeanour. They were far more rules and regulations orientated.

Day to day small talk was non-existent and telephone conversations were always kept to a minimum, with never any hint of humour. They were dedicated to the GN. The Midland was looked upon as the enemy and was never capable of doing anything correctly. This presumably was a throwback to the old pre-grouping or pre-nationalized days, or a grudge about the London Midland Region taking over what had been until recently Eastern Region territory.

241P that brought me from Paris on arrival at Rosporden. The junction for the metre gauge Reseau Breton. (Author)

4-6-0T-metre gauge mixed train for Carhaix. A stark contrast from the overnight 241P hauled express from Paris. (Author)

Merchant Navy 35007 Aberdeen Commonwealth awaits its next turn of duty at Weymouth MPD (Author)

Hopton Incline on the Cromford and High Peak (Author)

Reseau Breton Mallet being coaled. (Author)

Reseau Breton Mallet being turned at Carhaix (Author)

SNCF 231 pacific on Calais MPD (Author)

Kimberley retained its Class 2 status, having originally obtained it through its sheer volume of traffic, plus the operation of level crossing and wicket gates. Its Class 2 distinction was first obtained when coal traffic from the north Nottinghamshire and Derbyshire coalfields was at its height. General merchandise, especially beer from Burton on Trent, sugar beet, and grain transported from East Anglia had once made up its mainstay. Passenger services had disappeared in 1964 and all that remained in 1967 were some Belvoir-Stanton iron ore trains and a couple of Colwick East Yard to Horninglow Bridge (Burton-on-Trent) general freights. Motive power usually consisted of Class 20 or Class 25 diesels that were allocated to Toton.

Early and late turn shifts had about eight trains each, while the night shift had only one Burton-on-Trent freight. On occasion empty wagons from Stanton were sent to Bulwell Common for stabling, which gave the signalman at Bulwell and Basford Junction, the next box east to Kimberley, a chance to alter his points. This usually involved calling out the signal and telegraph department to fix and re-adjust them. However, the daily pick-up freight still ran from Colwick to Ilkeston North, the next box west to Kimberley. Ilkeston North box opened on a one shift basis between 0800-1600, Monday-Friday, and

MN 35013 Blue Funnel about to depart Southampton for Waterloo. (Author)

Stanton Junction the next box after Ilkeston North closed after the last Stanton – Belvoir iron stone train on Saturday lunchtime, until 0600 Mondays. It was then that Kimberley found itself working to

West Country Pacific 34056 Croydon awaiting departure for Weymouth. The Loco inspector leaning out of the cab refused my request for a footplate run! (Author)

Derby Friargate, or Eggington Junction – the latter being a very long section.

Because the working instructions at Kimberley had never been changed since Awsworth Junction closed, the signalman at Kimberley, when receiving the train entering section bell signal, was instructed to close the level crossing gates to road traffic and clear the home signal. The gradient of 1 in 40 approaching the signal was considered too steep for a train to start from a standstill, if stopped there. This may have been satisfactory when Awsworth was open as the section was only about a mile in length. But if one applied the working operations to the letter when working to Eggington Junction, road traffic could wait up to an hour! Kimberley was open from 0500 Monday to 2200 Saturday.

The daily pick-up to Ilkeston North was often used for transporting the p-way staff and any equipment needed. The p-way staff was made up of what appeared to be 'old retainers' resembling Dad's

Army who spent most of their working day either hiding in their cabin or drinking endless cups of tea in Kimberley, and other boxes along the line. They were all looking forward to the line finally closing and receiving their redundancy money.

The retired stationmaster from Kimberley station still lived in the stationmaster's house and kept 24-hour vigilance on the comings and goings of Kimberley box and its environment. It was his customary practice to arrive in the signal box at breakfast time, having first been alerted by the smell of the bacon and egg fry-up. He knew that a cup of tea or coffee would always be available and he still considered himself the station master.

By this time, Jim Barnes, and Cedric Pearson had taken over this section of the GN and were still the signalling inspectors. Walter Longland who had been the assistant area manager at Long Eaton had now become assistant area manager to John Brazier at Ilkeston North. So little change for me where

A Saturday morning 'Sortie' with Relief Signalman Ron Cox, Trent Relief Booking Clerk Alan Bowler, and now signalman Trent Junction, (ex Crescents Drummer) Bob Crew to photo one of the last Jubilees. 45562 Alberta is seen approaching Ambergate Station avoiding line with a S.O. New Street – Glasgow express. (Alan Bowler)

administration was concerned. Nottingham Control remained the same and I was still in contact with my old friends from the Trent and Toton area. Some relief signalmen from the Midland were learning boxes on the old GN, as many of the traditional signalmen off the GC, who would have relieved in the GN boxes, had taken early retirement when the GC main line was closed. Bob, Pinkie, Ron and of course Nigel still visited Kimberley. Nigel always arriving when there was the least activity.

Unauthorised visitors were the norm at Kimberley. These ranged from the village policemen, the retired railway man who couldn't leave the 'job' alone and the girlfriends of friends and colleagues. The latter were the most frowned upon by the retired stationmaster who never missed anything, relating what he had seen the following morning during his breakfast visits.

The main road through Kimberley passed under the railway line, while the original quieter

road passed over the line via the level crossing. Consequently, there was always a diversionary route for road traffic. Serious delays were unheard of for both road and rail. There were none of the fast freights or express passenger trains to worry about. In fact, Kimberley was very much like a 'retirement home for signalmen'. Most days were sedentary, and an evening stroll to the fish and chip shop and the Cricketers public house were mandatory. Kimberley was famed for its 'Kimberley Ale', brewed a couple of hundred yards from the box. It was customary for the late turn to buy a pint for the night turn signalman at the Cricketers and exchange turns of duty in the pub! Highly irregular. But then management didn't bother too much about the old GN and tended to lose themselves on the area whenever possible, often turning up at the pub at lunchtime.

At around 2000hrs it was normal to leave a 'line clear' to both Basford and Stanton Junction, so that should a train arrive at either of the two boxes, they

No. 45562. Alberta at Leeds. Note the yellow stripe on the cab side to identify not to go south of Crewe under the electrified overhead wires. (JR Carter)

could clear their signals for it to proceed towards Kimberley. This of course would give the Kimberley signalman 30 minutes' drinking time before returning to the box. One evening, while I was enjoying a second pint and convivial conversation around the bar at the Cricketers, the door burst open and a rather burly engine driver demanded, "Who is the bloody signalman?" I said that I was. He said, "I'm standing at your bloody signal and mine's a pint!" Another two pints later we returned to the box and the driver took his engine off to Colwick. No one was any the wiser.

Signalling was secondary to other activities at Kimberley. Reading, strolling around the town, playing my guitar and listening to pirate radio all seemed to occupy the early and late turn shift. Night shift was for sleeping. One could achieve five or six hours' quality sleep and therefore, could take full advantage of the daylight hours when one got home. This often involved meeting up with Ron, Bob, Pinkie and Nigel – the sole purpose to seek out the last remaining steam in and around Notts

and Derbyshire. These were often industrial locos. Collieries at Pinxton and William Thorpe, Cement and Gypsum works at Kelham, Langar, and Kegworth were all visited. Many a footplate run was achieved, especially at Pinxton and Sleights. Not quite the same as mainline steam, but nonetheless still an exhilarating experience. At least William Thorpe Colliery had some old BR tank engines that always seem to work in tandem.

Burning of the midnight oil took place on nights at Kimberley, thinking and planning being the order of the day. Where we should go, when we should go, and by what means. This latter decision was especially important for Nigel, as he was not entitled to free travel on BR. Saturday morning might see us at Ambergate to witness the Saturdays-only Birmingham to Glasgow express, usually hauled by one of the surviving Jubilees, normally 45562 *Alberta*. I later had the wonderful experience of riding the footplate of *Alberta* from Leeds to Carlisle shortly before she was withdrawn. She steamed well and

I was the envy of the numerous 'chuffer nutters' hanging out of the carriage windows.

Other morning sorties would see us on the Cromford and High Peak in Derbyshire, photographing the remaining ex WD J94's on the 1 in 13 Hopton Incline. Trips further afield were made, and twice we went across the Channel to France to photograph the last of French main line steam. Nigel only managed one trip due to financial restraints and time off from work. The French trips involved visiting Calais and Boulogne depots in search of steam, especially the pacifics that usually hauled the boat trains to Paris Nord.

We saw steam at Paris Bastille before it closed and also visited the Reseau Breton (Brittany Network) in Finistaire, Carhaix and Morlaix being two places that were a paradise for narrow gauge steam enthusiasts. Ron at that time contributed to the magazine *Narrow Gauge News* so the meter gauge lines that crossed Brittany were of considerable interest. Catching an overnight express to Rosporden and connecting into a meter gauge steam-hauled mixed train for Carhaix is an experience firmly engraved on my mind. We found on our arrival at Rosporden that a 2-4-1P steam loco had hauled our overnight express; and that unfortunately we had left the carriage window open and Ron had received a full frontal of smuts cascading from the engine during its journey.

Another trip was to Cormeilles on the outskirts of Paris where there was the vast cement works of Lambert Freres (Lambert Brothers). Lamberts cement works were famous for their narrow-gauge steam locos that spent their time pushing and pulling tub trucks around the worksites. This network had its own wagon and loco repair workshops where the staff welcomed us as though we were long lost relatives. Ron had visited there several times before and presented some of the drivers with photographs of their locos that he had taken on previous visits. These drivers looked upon us as complete eccentrics, but were always kindly disposed to our needs. It was here that I first found out that everything in France stops for two hours between noon and 2pm for lunch! These loco men invited us to take lunch with them, offering us wine and sharing their fromage and jambon. I have never subscribed to the English 'tabloid' view of the French, having always found them extremely kind, friendly and informed. I did however learn later that the Lambert Enterprise contributed towards the Front National political party of Jean-Marie Le Pen.

These were the halcyon days of my formative years, ones that could never be repeated or

Piggy in the middle 45675 Hardy on shed. (G McLean)

Alberta at Manchester Victoria nearing the end of her life. (RS Patterson)

forgotten. We were all getting older and more and more interested in the fairer sex. Somehow, the fairer sex did not always appreciate our railway interests and as we became more committed to our respective girlfriends, those interests had to take a back seat.

The S and T department were frequent visitors to Kimberley box. They drank copious amounts of coffee on the pretext of topping up the batteries under the box. These supplied the power source for the block signalling instruments and were fine GN examples that we signalmen kept highly polished.

Diesels take over at Carlisle. A sad day. (JG Glover)

Kimberley was quite luxurious compared to Midland boxes. It had running water, flush toilet, electric light and a comfortable armchair, ergonomic for sleeping. With a full 'head of steam' in the hearth and feet resting in the level crossing gate wheel, sleep was wonderful. However, one night the village 'bobby' pulled the level crossing gates out of their 'stops', thus spinning the gate wheel around with me firmly attached. He did thankfully rescue me from my unfortunate upside-down position! He was one of life's practical jokers. His other attempt to 'ruffle my feathers' was to creep up the box steps one night, while I was asleep, and place a huge rubber spider in my locker. I hate spiders. I went all night without a cup of tea! The early turn signalman removing the said spider on his arrival.

It was late afternoon one Friday that disaster struck. This was in the shape of Jim Barnes who had been visiting Midland boxes along the Erewash Valley. He had been passing the time of day in Bennerley Junction box. Bennerley Junction stood directly below Bennerley (GN) viaduct. This was situated between Ilkeston North and Kimberley.

Jim, relaxing in the signalman's chair, suddenly observed crossing the viaduct an engine and guards van heading towards Kimberley, closely followed by an empty iron ore train. Two trains in a section

was a cardinal sin! Jim departed Bennerley hot foot for Kimberley, arriving in a 'muck and fluster' for an explanation. This was left to me to fathom out and explain. Ilkeston North box had switched out some 20 minutes earlier. And it was there where the fault lay. It appeared that Ilkeston North switched out with the engine and guards van standing at the starting signal. Consequently, when the signalman switched out and closed his box, he cleared his signals, and the engine and guards van set off towards Kimberley.

I was unaware of the engine and guards van at Ilkeston. I was now switched through to Stanton Junction who had immediately offered me the iron ore empties! I was surprised to see the arrival of an engine and guards van instead of the iron ore empties, especially arriving in record time! Moments after the engine and guards van had arrived, the iron ore empties appeared in sight. This was closely followed by the sound of Jim Barnes racing up the box steps!

All became evident and the consequent result was that the regular signalman at Ilkeston was 'taken out' of the box and thus a vacancy appeared on the vacancy list. There were no takers for Ilkeston North. It was known as a 'bare week' box, or a 9-5 box with no overtime. Hence a basic wage. The box vacancy

BR Type 4 at Leeds with Thames-Clyde Express. (P Gerald)

was consequently covered by a relief signalman, which meant that our rest-days were invariably worked, as there was no relief signalman available for us to have time off. This was good for the pocket, but it did curtail days out.

As per usual practice, every Thursday a taxi arrived with the wages and any correspondence. This correspondence contained not only the vacancy lists as usual but also special train notices (STN) and the weekly engineering notices. Special trains were seldom seen at Kimberley. Trains appearing in the working timetable (WTT) were generally all we saw. The exceptions were a sugar beet specials from the Fens or petrol trains from Ellesmere Port.

It was one Saturday afternoon while most intermediate boxes were switched out that I received an express freight train from Eggington. I became worried that after one hour this train had not come into sight! I had had the crossing gates closed across the road for a good 30 minutes and received a fair amount of abuse from road users before they turned and took another route. Eventually there was a cloud of smoke towards Ilkeston and the Ellesmere Port tank train came into view hauled by a knackered old 8F. Why didn't

I have my camera? Signs of relief emanated from the driver and fireman, who were having some difficulty getting their loco to perform. Nonetheless it cleared Kimberley and Basford. The control in Nottingham said that once the engine returned from Colwick and cleared Eggington I could close and go home.

This was the first time I had seen steam at Kimberley and knowing that it was going to return I could telephone Nigel so that he too could witness this rare event. There was a telephone box near by and Nigel said he would be right over. True to his word, he arrived just after the 8F had disappeared out of view. Nigel had always had a habit of arriving late! We drowned his sorrows in the Cricketers after receiving 'train out of section' from Eggington and closing Kimberley until Monday.

Engineering work at Kimberley was rare as the line was subject to closure. Therefore, only basic maintenance work was carried out. This consisted of ballast tamping, or tunnel inspections. Single line working (SLW) was something I had managed to avoid. All of this was about to change as I had successfully applied for and got a Class 1 at Hasland Sidings.

CHAPTER 7

Hasland Sidings and Clay Cross North Signal Boxes

On hearing the news of my promotion, Plum concluded that I had gone completely insane! "What was wrong with that nice little signal box at Kimberley? Why on earth do you want go all the way to Chesterfield on that awful M1? You'll have to lodge near that new box. I'm sure you'll find some boarding house to stay in."

This was not my idea of living. A boarding house indeed! Plum did not understand that the old GN/GC was about to close, while all father could say was, "I hope you know what to you are doing boy and that you'll still get plenty of customers!" He related to all working activities in terms of customers and in this case he saw trains as my customers.

I had left Kimberley before the final curtain came down. Freight between Ilkeston Stanton Junction and Eggington Junction finished in May 1968, leaving just the Belvoir to Stanton iron ore stone traffic. This was to remain for only a short time until Nottingham Midland and the Erewash could route this.

I had difficulty finding Hasland Sidings box. It was situated along a dirt track that had until recently been the access to Hasland loco depot. This had been a freight sub-shed for a few locos required to work the colliery traffic around the Clay Cross and Chesterfield areas. Alas, now closed and all the buildings, with the exception of a few railway cottages, demolished. Hasland Sidings box was a forlorn sight. It was in a sorry state of repair; the paint that was left showed few traces of crimson lake maroon and cream.

It was situated alongside the Down main line, among a sea of dereliction. To compound all this, Avenue Coking Plant was directly behind the box and continuously belched out a yellow smoke, polluting the air and all vegetation. A thoroughly depressing part of the world.

Inside, the box faired little better than outside. Everything was either worn out or broken. The 'thunder box' (Elson chemical toilet) was full and blocked, the door to it broken, and the gas lighting in the box appeared somewhat dubious. Stores had never been ordered for any cleaning and it was only possible to see out of the windows at either end of the box. At the front it was impossible. Seeing Hasland Sidings for the first time I soon realised that no one in their right mind would have applied for the vacancy! Perhaps Plum had been correct in that I must be insane!

The other two incumbents were solitary individuals. One signalman continually repaired and serviced motorbikes in the box, leaving parts soaking in the filthy butler sink. This at least accounted for the neglected state of the box. The other was a somewhat dour and monosyllabic character that took great delight in arriving at the exact minute he was to take up duty. He walked from home, one of the railway cottages a mile away, and had timed his daily trek to the last second.

The rotary block signalling instruments were forever causing problems They seldom worked correctly and the S & T (signal and telegraph) department had to be called out to attend. As the S & T were always where they were unobtainable, they inherited the derivation of both 'sick and tired' or 'sit and talk'! They did however show me how to fix the problem, unofficially of course. This involved a little dismantling of the instrument! All highly irregular, but evidently a well-known practice in many boxes.

The regular signalmen at Hasland Sidings, and adjoining boxes Horns Bridge and Avenue Sidings, found it hard to believe that I had been appointed a Class 1 at the tender age of 20. Most of the signalmen along this stretch of the Erewash were considerably older than signalmen further south in the Toton and Trent area. They often appeared stuck in their ways, tending to be somewhat parochial. Nonetheless,

Jubilee 45593 Kolhapur on the up goods line at Hasland Sidings. The vast expanse in the background is where once stood Hasland MPD. (Author)

I was accepted eventually as the new kid on the block and was highly honoured to join the Thursday evening 'booze cruise' when we were all working the early turn. This involved several of us piling into two cars and sampling the country pubs around Ashover, Stretton and Clay Cross.

Drink driving law was something yet to arrive. Anyway, most signalmen had a good relationship with the local constabulary who turned a blind eye. We all contributed 10/- for these expeditions and whatever was left went towards the petrol. We took it in turn to share driving duties, or whoever was the most capable got the job of driving everyone home. The hours normally spent talking on the open

telephone system became an exception on Friday mornings when we were all feeling a little fragile.

I took Plum's advice and moved out of the parental home in Bramcote. This was something I should have done years before. My new abode was a small bedsitter in a terraced house in Chesterfield. At last I was free of the austerity cooking of Plum and could indulge myself with the cuisine from Chinese and Indian takeaways. I also had privacy and no longer had to entertain girls in the restricted space of a Morris 1000! However, I did have to share the bathroom with the other inhabitants on the same floor: a single parent, and to me it was obvious as to why she was single, and an aspiring opera singer.

original toiletry procedure! Meanwhile I rescheduled my visit, shortening it by a couple of days!

My return to Chesterfield was on the footplate of a Class 45 diesel hauling the St Pancras-Glasgow sleeper from Nottingham via Derby. On leaving Derby the fog came down and we were seeing fog hand signalmen on the ground repeating appropriate aspects of the signals they stood beside. On approaching Ambergate we were abruptly confronted with the three red lights of a goods guards van immediately in front of us! The driver, being unconcerned, continued at line speed while I had palpitations! We passed the offending guards van and its train in the adjoining loop, sounding a wake-up warning to the guard. The driver said it was quite normal for guards to fall asleep and forget to change the red lamp to white nearest the main line, when they were on an adjacent line. I think I aged by several years that night.

The winter brought heavy snow and my newly acquired Vauxhall Viva was no match for the snowy, damp conditions. The slightest sign of damp and it refused to start. It spent most of its time outside Hasland Sidings awaiting a dry, sunny day, so that it could be moved. My car had clearly been made either on a Friday evening or a Monday morning. It caused me more problems financially than I had ever encountered before. I was often late on duty thanks to it, and had to walk either to or from the box in the rain. I eventually traded it in against an elderly VW Beetle and declared that I would never buy another Vauxhall.

Car problems over, life became less stressful. The box was starting to look more like it was cared for, and although the traffic density was far greater than that of Kimberley, with close to 100 trains a shift, life was very pleasurable. The pollution from the coking plant was beginning to tell on me however. It was making me feel sick and my food tasted of chemicals. Perhaps this was a forerunner to the industrial junk food served up many years later by McDonalds.

Nigel's visits were less frequent, although he did arrive one day in his newly acquired Austin-Healey Sprite sports car. This refused to start when he wanted to leave and the AA was called out to rectify the fault. They came eventually; long after all hope of them arriving had faded. Nigel did witness most of the night shift at Hasland Sidings as consolation.

During one of Nigel's visits, it was decided that a couple of days spent on the Southern Region, around the New Forest, might not go amiss. The purpose of this was to witness the last of steam on the main line from London Waterloo. The date set, off we went in the Sprite. After a cold and uncomfortable car journey we arrived in Brockenhurst. We achieved a footplate run on Merchant Navy Class locomotive *Aberdeen Commonwealth* to Weymouth on the Channel Islands Boat Express. The evening was stormy and lightning silhouetted the Purbeck Hills.

Christmas came and Hasland was closed for a few days; my shift fell correctly for me to have a longer Christmas than most railway shift workers. I foolishly went to see the parents, taking father his Christmas present – an electric shaver. This turned out to be a disaster on Boxing Day, when all of a sudden there was an enormous bang from the kitchen fuse box. Evidently father had lathered his face as normal for his morning shave then used the new electric razor. This completely 'clagged up' the mechanism so he then put it in the wash basin to clean it, all without disconnecting it from its power supply and thus rendering it useless. Plum looked to the heavens in despair and father returned to his

The train called at Wool, stopping directly in front of the signal box, blocking the level crossing. From the footplate the signal box looked most inviting, as the locomotive must have done for those waiting in their cars at the crossing. The firebox glow and drifting steam of this majestic and beautiful machine created a dramatic atmosphere.

Photographs and paintings could never do justice to this experience. The thrill of a rough and bumpy ride on a Merchant Navy pacific over jointed track at 85mph descending Bincombe bank, with the lights of Weymouth looking closer than they actually were, made me consider my mortality. Excess speed that night by the driver was to ensure a pint at the Weymouth BRSA (British Railways Staff Association Club) before last orders were called. We returned on the footplate of a much newer BR standard Class 5 locomotive.

Instead of getting off at Brockenhurst we stayed on the footplate to Waterloo. The Nine Elms-based driver taking the train forward to London was extremely good-natured, and we took advantage of this, arriving in Waterloo at dawn. We decided to find Stewarts Lane loco depot but managed to take the wrong underground train, ending up at Kensington Olympia. This virtually unknown station had a host of ex Great Western (GW) signals and ex London and North Western (LNW) signal boxes. It had access to all four regions of BR yet it appeared to be a little used cross London route. Its track layout consisted of an extremely fascinating configuration and especially interesting were the lengthy platforms, all fully signalled. Every signalling permutation had been considered. We did not see any trains though! Little did I realise that some year's later destiny would take me back to Kensington.

But first we had to get back to Brockenhurst, preferably avoiding buying a ticket! Purchasers of platform tickets were scrutinized at the ticket barrier and consequently Nigel paid up for the return. I was a little more fortunate in having my free pass, which always bugged Nigel. I did help Nigel out sometimes and bought the odd beef burger at the proverbial Wimpy bar, even though Nigel once had an altercation with a tomato-shaped sauce bottle, which he successfully managed to explode across our and adjoining tables. This resulted in us being jettisoned from the establishment 'tout de suite', and supposedly banned from all Wimpy bars.

The next couple of days were spent sampling beer and photographing the diminishing steam scene around Wool, Dorchester, Moreton and Sway. We visited Weymouth loco shed and saw our old 'friend' *Aberdeen Commonwealth*. In daylight she was in a sorry condition, with many steam pipes around the footplate held together with string. She was in a filthy state but she was in steam, and programmed to work a Waterloo express later that day.

We returned back to the Midlands in the unfortunate Sprite, via the preserved Bluebell Railway, and in so doing ended up going along a dual carriageway in the wrong direction. Oh the joys of driving. Poor Nigel never got over that – I believe it was his first driving mishap.

There were a few instances when steam appeared at Hasland Sidings, but sadly none of these appearances were dramatic. Alan Pegler's *Flying Scotsman* conveyed an enthusiast special northwards on one occasion. This I managed to stop at the home signal to get a decent photo, once it restarted!

It's easier to be granted forgiveness than to be granted permission, thought I.

Comrades Pinkie, Bob, and Ron had all moved on. Pinkie was now relief signalman at Trent, Bob had gone to Long Eaton Junction and Ron installed at Trent Station North Junction. Alan Bullimore had gone to Stanton Gate and although we saw each other far less we still kept in touch via 'the speaking wire' (the internal telephone). Mac had gone to work for a 'bookmakers' for a short time before rejoining the world of pop groups.

Rumours were rife. The Midland line through the Derbyshire Peak district, via Millers Dale, was due to close with the St Pancras-Manchester trains being rerouted via the Erewash, and the Hope Valley. Redundancies were a reality now, with displaced signalmen becoming guards, or worse still being transferred to the p-way. Some signalmen from Matlock, Darley Dale and Bakewell managed a short stay transfer to the Erewash, while some from the former line through the north Derbyshire Dales went to vacancies along the Hope Valley. I still had ambition and wanted to earn £1,000 a year (£20 a week). I applied for a sideways move from one Class 1 box to another: Clay Cross North Junction. Clay Cross North Junction was one of the most interesting boxes along the Erewash and was also a 'money box'. Plenty of overtime! I was tired of the just Up and Down monotony of Hasland Sidings, and the putrid smell from the coking plant. The pollution was so severe that even the houses downwind of the yellow smog had to have rags firmly placed in their letterboxes to stop the smell entering their homes. There was little environmental control in the 60s.

Clay Cross North Junction had the luxury of a train regulator and thus both roles became (unofficially) shared. I successfully reached the zenith of my Erewash days at Clay Cross North, but not before my first real encounter with a 'graduate' inspector.

This was at Hasland Sidings during an engineer's possession. The Up main had been taken over by the engineers between Horns Bridge and Hasland Sidings for 'tamping and consolidation' of the ballast. Hasland Sidings therefore received all trains on the Up goods line, and then turned them out to Up main line, and thus regaining there booked route. As the Newcastle-Bristol sleeper and mail train was crossing from the Up goods to the Up main a tamping machine came past the Up main home signal at danger and continued on its collision course towards the Bristol mail! I immediately exhibited a red hand signal and fortunately both the Bristol mail and the tamping machine stopped. This resulted in an altercation with the inspector on the tamping machine who had absolutely zero knowledge about what he was doing. The driver of the Bristol mail, the Clay Cross regulator and myself gave him a dressing down he would never forget. The sad thing is he didn't know what he had done wrong. Many of these 'graduate' failures moved on quite quickly, gaining promotion in another area. No doubt they arrived at their new domain highly recommended. It was hard to believe that these recruits were to be the future for the rail industry. Was it time for me to consider a career change?

Signalmen tend to be solitary individuals who would probably be just as happy being a lighthouse keeper. Visitors to their boxes, unless invited, were looked upon as an intrusion on their privacy, especially the p-way flagman during engineering possessions. They would take over the box for most of the shift. Senior managers were usually interesting conversationalists and personable, while the new breed of inspectors were usually arrogant and out to score 'brownie points'. These were always looking at ways to catch you out. Inspectors made random checks on the train register book. This was to ensure that all the entries were correct and that the times entered corresponded with those entered in the adjoining boxes.

Senior relief signalmen sometimes deputised for the signalling inspector on these duties and often 'covered up' any irregularities. Relief signalmen were also used on 'pilotmen' duties during Single Line Working (SLW). The pilotman being responsible for authorising movement on or off the single line while the opposite or adjoining line was blocked for engineering purposes. This always upset the normal running and caused many problems for all involved. In general, upheaval of the norm. Every Thursday one would look at the engineering notices to see if one's own box was to be involved in SLW or worse still some mammoth track relaying work.

Until my move to Clay Cross North, I had managed to avoid most of the significant p-way work that many of my signalling colleagues had endured. Alas, the threat we had dreaded was fast approaching. Time was running out. Trent Power signal box was approaching. All boxes between Loughborough and Horns Bridge (Chesterfield) were to be taken over by one Power Signal Box (PSB).

Due to the increase in road freight thanks to the cozy relationship between Minister of Transport and road hauliers, rail freight traffic was slowly being eroded. Consequently, many sidings and additional running lines were being ripped up.

There was a complete rationalisation programme afoot which helped make the PSB territory simpler to implement and operate. Double track junctions were to be simplified and made into single track, or lead, junctions composed of a series of crossovers. This may have been satisfactory for the lesser-used junction where only one train at a time traversed it, but for the busier junction where it was necessary, due to traffic density, for two trains to pass simultaneously, this form of rationalisation was operational suicide. Rationalisation at junctions also posed a huge problem for the timetable planners, requiring them to allow more recovery time that consequently caused a general slow down of the network. These plans, and their implementation, became the topic of conversation on the open circuit telephone.

The nighttime conversation covered the which, when and who. This related to which boxes were to close, and which might remain as a 'fringe' to the new PSB, and of course when was it going to happen and who was going to remain. Who was the most senior? And what was the timescale? The most important aspect was, what was going to happen to so many of us signalmen?

The area manger at Westhouses announced vacancies for guards, and we learned that some boxes would remain, at least for the short term as fringe boxes, until Sheffield PSB was implemented. The boxes that would remain on what was still known as the Nottingham Division were Loughborough, Lock Lane Crossing (control of barriers), Long Eaton Station my old haunt (control of barriers), Stapleford and Sandiacre (a double-manned shunting frame for access to and from Toton Diesel Depot) Stanton Gate, Alan Bullimore's domain (to become a shunting frame handling the traffic that once used the GN via Kimberley) and Horns Bridge. Several boxes along the Pye Bridge to Mansfield line would remain with Sleights becoming the fringe box. Stretton was to remain on the Derby line.

During this period much engineering took place. SLW and diversions of traffic became common practice every weekend.

Clay Cross North Junction was an interesting box to work, with most of the regulating taking place for the Derby and west of England lines and the Midland main line along the Erewash. It was imperative to know the point-to-point timings in order that a slow-moving train would not impede a faster moving one. The train regulator was a great help in this area as he was in constant communication with all the boxes to Pye Bridge Junction, where another train regulator was installed for regulating south of Pye Bridge. Tapton Junction, north of Chesterfield, still had a box lad. Control reporters was never a term used for box lads on the Eastern Region. The Eastern Region boundary started halfway between Hasland Sidings and Horns Bridge. The Eastern

Region had always considered itself superior to the Midland Region, and the Midland Region considered itself likewise to the Eastern Region.

Gordon, the train regulator on my shift at Clay Cross, was an ex-signalman from Barrow Hill. He had a good sense of humour, and he was the most capable of all the regulators. He never once got it wrong. He was also a very proficient signalman and I could eat my meals without any fears of the 'job' going to 'pot'. Gordon also joined us on the Thursday evening booze cruises.

It was on one late-turn (2-10) just as I went off duty that news came in of a derailment between Wingfield and Crich Junction. A train conveying 100-ton petrol tanks had become derailed on the Up main line half way between the two boxes. The Control, in Nottingham, suggested I should go there and implement single line working (SLW) over the Down line. I agreed, thinking more of the overtime than the practicality. I arrived at Wingfield and was pleased to find that there was already a responsible officer in charge of the incident. He had instigated SLW but was awaiting my arrival as pilotman to authorise or accompany trains on and off the single line. The only train to cross over from the Up to the Down and conduct through to Crich was the Newcastle-Bristol

Having 'taken authority' I unofficially stopped Flying Scotsman at Hasland in order to take this photo! Sadly not the dramatic photo I had wanted. (Author)

mail and sleeper. I was to return on a Curzon Street (Birmingham)-Sheffield parcels train. After which, total possession of both lines would be taken by the engineers so that the BDVs (break down vans) could re-rail the offending tank wagon.

Soon after my arrival the Newcastle-Bristol showed up. I informed the driver, who I soon found out was the second man (driver's assistant), that he must draw his train forward clear of the crossover and then reverse back through the crossover onto the down line. I would accompany him through the section. All went well. I climbed onto the footplate of the Class 45 diesel and found that the driver was fast

asleep in the second man's seat on the other side of the footplate. Under the seat was a case of Newcastle Brown Ale. The driver awoke and immediately offered me a bottle. All very generous, but highly irregular. We continued 'bang road' (facing direction) past the derailed train and eventually crossed over to the correct running line at Crich Junction. I bid my farewell and immediately climbed aboard a Class 25 diesel hauling the Curzon Street-Sheffield parcels train for the return journey.

This was my baptism for SLW. I was still on a high when I eventually got home. The adrenalin buzz taking some time to disappear. I got four hours' overtime at a higher rate of pay plus petrol.

Rationalisation, modernisation, demoralisation all progressed rapidly. The railways I had known and loved were fast changing for the worse. The morale, motivation and the camaraderie were fast disappearing. It was time to change. Clay Cross North would soon be no more, although Avenue Sidings box suddenly got a reprieve in the overall scheme of things, getting reduced from a signal box to shunting frame status to handle arrivals destined for the dreaded coking plant.

The remainder of us signalmen diversified. Pinkie still remained a signalman, but changed his location to Loughborough. Bob went to work at the family printing business and Ron went to the new PSB. Ron did however have an unfortunate experience towards the end of the manual signaling days. He was on night turn of duty at Stanton Gate South when he received the emergency bell signal 4-5-5 (train or vehicles running away on the right line) from the signalman at Stanton Gate North, just as he was crossing a slow freight train from the second Down goods line across the main lines to the first Down goods line.

The 4-5-5 emergency bell signal that Ron received at Stanton Gate South was for the Leeds-Leicester express freight on the Up main line. There was no time to act, Stanton Gate North being just over a quarter of a mile away. Ron however did manage to send six bells (the emergency bell signal for obstruction danger) to boxes both north and south before the impact, which was directly in front of Stanton Gate South box. No harm befell Ron (other than shock) or the box but sadly the driver of the Leeds-Leicester lost his life and the debris was strewn around all of the running lines for a significant distance. The subsequent inquiry revealed that the driver had been asleep at his controls for some considerable time. His progress had been recorded in the train register books in all the boxes from as far north as Pye Bridge Junction. It revealed excessive speed and that he had ignored all speed restrictions. Ron would certainly be safer in the confines of Trent PSB!

For my part, well, I resigned and pursued the only other career I knew: music!

PART TWO

CHAPTER 8

The Rock Management and Agency Years in Soho

I t was back in Nottingham that I met 'Lebbo'. He was an excellent and inspirational guitarist and prolific songwriter. He resembled an eccentric hippy or author. He played in a three-piece 'progressive rock band' called 'BOMB' (Band of Mental Breakdown). The term 'band' had superseded 'group' by now, and groups were no longer called 'The' something or other, as they were in the days of my own group The Crescents a decade before. BOMB's musical synergy and their playing ability made me want to give up my guitar forever. I was hooked.

Like most aspiring musicians, they were short of both money and transport. Contacts were also hard for them to come by. However, I had the contacts from the days of The Crescents and was prepared to chance a few bob on them becoming a success. So, loaded up in a VW Dormobile we set off to a rented cottage in Somerset, appropriately near Glastonbury, with the sole aim of 'getting it together'. Musically that is. The idea was we would emerge after a period of time and take the London rock scene by storm.

Although I had always had a fondness for Somerset, somehow the Somerset levels around Street, Wells and Glastonbury were not so pleasing to the eye as North Somerset around Minehead. Fond memories of trainspotting in this neck of the woods would have to remain just a memory. Sadly, the old S & D (Somerset and Dorset) Railway line from Bath Green Park was now closed, but the village pub was still called The Railway Inn, minus proximity to any rails. It was at the Railway Inn that BOMB rehearsed. The landlady being extremely sympathetic to our cause may have had something to do with her desire to sell more beer. Or more particularly, cider – the rough cider brewed locally and fermented in rats' tails. The latter was very strong and the effects when one went out into the fresh night air could result in some strange sensations. Many were the times we staggered back to the cottage.

Me. 'The Pop Impresario'. (Author)

The local 'agency' and promoter in nearby Street was reluctant to offer us work. Although he used to promote well-known pop groups and Radio One DJs, we were seldom offered any supporting role. The weekly music paper or bible for all aspiring bands was *Melody Maker*, and it was through the 'gig' list advertising 'What's On' that we pinned our hopes of any recognition. The top venues in London were the Marquee Club and the Temple Club, both situated on Wardour Street. The Temple Club ran all nighters

T2

Sole Representation:

T2. Andy Bown (lead guitar), Pete Dunton (drums and vocals), John Weir (bass). (Author)

on Friday and Saturday nights. Doors opened at 9pm and everyone got kicked out (literally) at 6am. During those nine hours three bands (two supporting bands and a top act band) appeared. The top band, or top of the bill, appeared at 1am. They were sandwiched between the two support bands that appeared at 11pm and 3am respectively. As so-called manager of BOMB, it was up to me to secure a London gig – the launch being intended to attract a recording contract and stardom.

Thin Lizzy in 1971. (Ted Carroll)

After several visits to London, I succeeded in arranging a support spot for BOMB at the Temple Club. Fee £5. The equipment was to arrive at 6pm, as was the equipment of the other two groups. Contracts for the performance were exchanged and the £5 fee would be paid within seven days by Nucleus Agency. We invited several representatives from record companies to see BOMB and we eagerly awaited the edition of *Melody Maker* to see BOMB's name among the great names of rock. BOMB was to be supporting a fairly well-known progressive rock band called Bram Stoker. We had seen their name many times in *Melody Maker* and we were very excited about appearing on the same bill as them. Another support band called Nothing Ever Happens, from Hull, were also booked to appear on the same bill.

The big day came and we arrived on Wardour Street at 6pm. So had Bram Stoker and Nothing Ever

Happens. We had arrived in the VW Dormobile while the others had arrived in hired Luton trucks. They had roadies to transport their equipment down the narrow stairwell whereas we did all the humping and dumping ourselves. Their band members were nowhere to be seen and would no doubt arrive 30 minutes before their performance. As the poor relation, all we could do was to hang about in Soho.

The Temple Club was a dim cavernous cellar painted black with red doors. The ceiling had cylindrical pipes that were air vents for the club, and the heating system (possibly gas) for the Chinese restaurant next door and the Whisky A Go Go nightclub above. The stage was about 7m by 5m and had to contain the equipment for all three bands. It was essential that the stage manager coordinated this well.

In addition to the bands' equipment, one had to consider the kit of the liquid wheel projection lighting team and that of the resident DJ, Jerry Floyd. Jerry was London's top DJ. He was one of the few in his trade who could assess an atmosphere with his choice in music and create an ambiance. He was capable of playing the correct music before and after the band so that it would complement their performance. He was the ideal linkman. His choice of music was diverse and he would introduce the bands with some knowledge gleaned beforehand, however unknown the bands may have been. He was a true professional and I was privileged to work with him later in my life. Jerry had several boxes of discs, mainly LPs, and these were the responsibility of his roadie, Paddy. Subsequently, it was total panic between 6pm and 9pm until the club opened.

The Temple Club did not sell alcohol; Fanta orange, coke, milk and hamburgers were all that was available. And there was only one entrance, which was extremely narrow. It led to a narrow staircase where carrying any form of musical equipment was difficult. It was impossible to pass anyone coming in the opposite direction. The timings for the bands rested with the stage manager and the preference of the star or top of the bill band. Of course, the

number of 'punters' arriving was very much down to the popularity, or the pulling power, of the top band.

BOMB was first to perform at 11pm. They were scheduled for a 60-minute session. Bram Stoker followed at 1am and Nothing Ever Happens at 3am. It only left one hour to change all the equipment between performances. This is no easy feat as the equipment from the first band had to be carried out through the auditorium across punters lying sprawled in heaps on the floor, up the stairs and loaded back into the van on Wardour Street. This manoeuvre had to be done quickly in so that the next band could arrange their equipment.

Soho is not a very salubrious area at the best of times and seemed to take on a menacing air in the small hours. This task of removing the equipment after the performance was made doubly hard for Bram Stoker as they had a Hammond organ!

BOMB set up their equipment at the front of the stage with the other two bands' equipment tightly packed behind. I had prepared a 'guest list' that contained the great and good from the recording world. This I presented to the doorman/bouncer and he introduced himself as 'Bigger'. He resembled

Flying Hat Band. Glen Tipton (guitar and vocals), Trevor 'Fozz' Foster (drums), Andy Wheeler (bass). (George Toone)

Marquee Club on Wardour Street. Every night hundreds of rock fans queued up outside to see the top bands of the day. (Alamy)

'Oddjob' in the James Bond movies. He was also the bouncer for the Whisky A Go Go upstairs and Charlie Chester's club when required.

The Whisky A Go Go was an all-night disco-come-pick-up-joint selling synthetic booze and frequented by 'ladies of the night', while Chester's was a gaming club. Senior police officers mingled with the criminal underworld in equal numbers, frequenting all three of these venues. There was good rapport between the underworld and the police. It was difficult for someone like me 'up from the sticks' to equate to this and it was a real eye-opener to both BOMB and I. The police hob-knobbing with known criminals! We were very unworldly in those days. In fact, extremely naive.

Punters were few as it turned out and BOMB played their set to only 20 people. The audience consisted of hippies in Afghan coats high on cannabis, speed or LSD. They danced around in singular fashion, silhouetted by the liquid wheel projection. The only people listening to BOMB were Jerry and I. A ripple of applause followed their set and no one mentioned on the guest list showed up. We did, however, meet an upmarket hippy called Harvey. Smartly dressed, he had associations with De Lane Lea recording studios. We were convinced that he sold drugs, but it seemed everyone did at the Temple Club. The police, knowing this, kept a low profile and were only interested if any 'pushers' appeared on Wardour Street. They were content knowing that all the 'druggies' were together in one place, and that while they were there no harm could be done. The police who did appear during the night were only interested in young 'run-aways'. We treated everyone with suspicion in Soho.

Harvey promised to keep in touch with a view to BOMB making a demo disc and we stuck around to watch Bram Stoker. They were excellent and had managed to attract a few more punters. We had a brief word with them before we left for the journey back to Somerset. They were based in the Bournemouth and Poole area, and just the mention of those towns reminded me of Merchant Navy pacific locomotives hauling the Channel Islands Boat Express to Weymouth. A far cry from the sordid world of Wardour Street.

Crestfallen, we arrived back in Somerset. And a few days later Harvey appeared. We rehearsed back

at the Railway Inn, but somehow the adrenalin and the motivation was not the same. BOMB called it a day and returned to Nottingham. Harvey and I set off in the Dormobile to Birmingham where Harvey decided to stay with a friend. Meanwhile, I carried on to London.

I arrived in London and went to Nucleus Agency, thinking they might be sympathetic to my cause. I wanted employment in the 'business' – it fascinated me. Stuart, the boss at Nucleus offered me the position of agency booker and said I could start the next day!

Nucleus was the agency that booked the Temple Club and represented artists who recorded on the Ember label. Their best-known band was Blonde on Blonde, who had had a mediocre hit with Castles in the Sky after they had appeared at the Bob Dylan Isle of White Festival.

John Mayall and his Bluesbreakers were regulars at the Marquee. Every rock musician played in the Bluesbreakers in the early 60s. It was like work experience before making it big in the world of rock. (Alamy)

Having started out as Hocus Pocus, changing their name to UFO helped make them rock superstars – firstly in Germany then Japan and finally in the USA and the UK. The late Pete Way, bass guitarist and railway enthusiast friend, is second from the right. (Alamy)

I had previously been to the Red Bus Agency seeking some form of employment but without much success. However, a Lindsey Brown offered me digs in a house at Acton with the band he managed called Flying Fortress. This I accepted. The Red Bus Agency handled Mungo Gerry and a band called Comus. They were also the agency for Lindsey's band, and Lindsey thought that if I was at Nucleus I could no doubt get Flying Fortress work. While Nucleus booked the Temple, Red Bus booked many of the prestige universities and Lindsey had inroads to the Marquee Club. You scratch my back and I'll scratch yours, sprung to mind.

There was a certain amount of snobbishness among the London Agencies. They were very competitive; very secretive about venues and fees. There were a lot of 'back-handers' to entertainment secretaries at the universities. There was also an amount of buying and selling of a band. This would involve a promoter (often an agent) buying a band or artist for a week at an arranged fee, and then selling each day of the week to separate venues and doubling the money. The artist had no idea what fee they were working for. Agents and managers representing the really big attractions would seldom quote a fee when enquiries were made, saying that their act was not available. The management, recognising that a market existed in that town or area where the enquiry came from, then promoted the concert themselves!

I arrived at Nucleus the following morning at nine o'clock, not realising that in the entertainment world nothing starts until after ten. Sandra was the secretary who hailed from Canada, while Ron completed the team. Ron was manager of a band called Warhorse, an offshoot from Deep Purple, led by their ex-bass guitarist Nick Simper. Warhorse had just released their first album and single (St Louis) on the Vertigo label. Everything at Nucleus was now geared around Warhorse. Blonde on Blonde took second place, while excitement was being generated by new arrival UFO. UFO had been signed to the Ember label and had great success in Germany and Japan with top 10 hits in both countries. Sadly, they were not quite so successful in the UK

It was much later in Germany that I witnessed first hand the enormous success of UFO.

Wolfgang Hawuge, a German promoter had arranged a concert in Whuppertal, in what could best be described as a football stadium with a roof. On arrival we had police escorts and police guards outside our hotel. We were quite overwhelmed by the fans and wished we had demanded a higher fee. We were interviewed on German Television – this all being a far cry from the £75 a night gigs in seedy venues in the UK with little attention from the media. It gave UFO a taste of things to come later still in Japan when they played stadiums in Tokyo and Osaka, also later when they conquered America and gained superstar status. It was some years after that they gained acclaim in the UK.

My role was to expose bands signed to, or about to be signed to the agency, and attain gigs at the top venues across the UK. This was made easier if a band had backing from their record company or had a record in the charts and receiving airtime on commercial radio or Radio One. Press articles and features, especially in *Melody Maker*, *Sounds*, and *NME* (*New Musical Express*) played a vital role in a band's success. The journalist Chris Welch who wrote for *Melody Maker* was considered a guru in the world of pop and rock. Chris's weekly fly on the wall article 'Caught in the Act' could create or decimate a band. Nonetheless, Chris got it right, and bands would always hope that Chris would appear at their gigs.

Sensuous ladies were employed by managers of bands as 'record pluggers' to persuade Radio and TV programme producers to give airtime to their bands. Their fee was about £50 a play on Radio One and £100 for Disco Two or Top of the Pops. Shortly after one 'plugger' had left our office, Arabella Ponsonby-Codpiece (or similar sounding name) telephoned from the BBC to say that Warhorse was to appear on Disco Two the next day! She demanded, most assertively, that they should arrive with their hair washed. The 'Beeb' somehow managed to employ society oddballs. How this record plugger procured her results we shall never know, and we certainly never asked! 'Payola' was very topical at that time,

as was 'fixing' the top 40. It was very important that newly released singles, or albums, should gain a top 40 entry.

The record charts were compiled from the sales of only about a dozen record shops across the UK. Therefore, if one knew where these shops were, then 'hey-presto!' A top 40 hit! Warhorse did enter the top 40 after their TV appearance and their date sheet of gigs became a lot healthier. It could be alleged that management and group members bought the lion's share of their single, St Louis!

Getting gigs for bands was quite an easy task at Nucleus as there were constant enquiries from local agencies all over the UK wanting to get their unknown bands a gig at the Temple Club. This was usually agreed if they sent in a suitable demo tape and arranged a gig for a Nucleus band in their neck of the woods. If an unknown band appeared at the Temple, they received £5. For a second appearance £10, and for a third appearance £15. The top of the bill would normally receive a guaranteed fee or 60% of the door take, whichever was the greater. Some top bands would receive as much as £500!

Because Nucleus had sole agency of the Temple Club I was expected to ensure all went well with the bands every weekend. Thus, I became not only an agent during the week but a stage manager at weekends. I had first opportunity to see any new up and coming band.

Daytimes were spent in Nucleus, while evenings were spent visiting venues to see bands, often with Lindsey from Red Bus. One venue Lindsey booked was Ewell Tech. He had been an entertainments secretary for the student union some years before and consequently knew the ropes. Entertainments secretaries were the privileged few and they drove hard bargains.

I saw Thunderclap Newman and Family at Ewell Tech. Both were good bands but lacked a certain sparkle. They were like many of the progressive bands at the time, being rather self-indulgent. Overly long guitar solos which either sent one off to the bar or put one to sleep. Only those who thought themselves a part of the music intelligentsia had the patience to see the complete set. 'I've suffered for my art, now it's your turn!' Is a phrase that springs to mind.

Nucleus soon started to promote bands on Sunday lunchtimes at the Marquee Club and all-nighters at the Lyceum Ballroom on the Strand. I was now far more involved than I had ever envisaged on that first day when I crossed the threshold of Nucleus.

It was in the Marquee Club's dressing room I first sampled a 'joint'. Humble Pie were waiting their entrance and were busy consuming the mandatory brandy that all rock musicians carried around in their guitar cases, when I noticed a rather large hand rolled cigarette being passed around. I was naïve. After all, I was the son of an aspiring retailer and had been schooled at the school for gentle folk. I was from the 'sticks'. But I soon realised that I must either accept or refuse this when passed to me.

Fearing that I would become a social outcast, I accepted the peer-group pressure, inhaled, and thought very little of it, feeling nothing. The cigarette came around again. Again I inhaled, and again I felt nothing. It was only when I went out front into the audience to watch the group that I felt different. Time passed slowly, as if in slow motion, and I could pick out each instrument in the band clearly.

I now fully understand how great musicians managed to perform the impossible, and how songwriters have written such wonderful pieces. Either dope- or booze-assisted!

Nucleus promoted many top groups at the Lyceum; Slade, Genesis, Steamhammer, Audience, Steeleye Span, Fleetwood Mac, Coliseum, If and Curved Air are just some of the groups I always remember. It was all work and no play with little opportunity to see trains that I then felt was my true passion. I did, however, travel by rail whenever possible and had the pleasure one late night of seeing a London Transport steam engine (an ex-Great Western pannier tank) hauling a London Transport engineering ballast train on the District line. I thought I was hallucinating, or I had smoked too much, but no, it was real. The sound and the smell of steam all helped bring back childhood memories.

Nucleus had been the brainchild of Geoff Kruger, the supremo behind Sparta Florida Music, the music-publishing house for Frank Sinatra, Glen Campbell and a host of artists recording on the Ember label. Their headquarters were at the Carlton Tower on Sloane Street, while the main activity took place at a beautiful house on Lisle Street. I often worked from there and fell in love with that part of London. I must have been impressed with wealth and glamour. Then at the age of 24, it was easy to be impressed. The trappings of wealth and so-called success were what I wanted. This came pretty quickly as I was soon well into the mainstream of the business. I was living life in the fast lane, much of which was thanks to the Temple Club and its many contacts. The rock business was one big network. Back scratching and backbiting were the norm. I soon learned never to trust other agents. They either wanted your acts or sole agency for your venues. Nice to your face, but behind your back – unscrupulous!

Two bands who appeared at the Temple club and later attained superstar status were Thin Lizzy and Flying Hat Band. These were both hard-hitting 3-piece bands. I found them most exciting. No doubt a throwback from my Crescents days. I firmly believe, that a three-piece line-up gives a clearer, more gutsy sound than that of a four-instrument line-up.

Flying Hat Band, a Birmingham Black Sabbath type of band eventually split up and the lead guitarist Glenn Tipton went with Judas Priest. Glenn became the main lynchpin in Judas Priest. He was personable and unassuming; he never became conceited, in spite of his extraordinary talent, unlike many other rock stars. Thin Lizzy went on to dominate the charts until the untimely death of their front man Phil Lynott. Phil told me he had been most surprised at his success being both black and Irish. He had a good sense of humour and no doubt shared this with his father-in-law, the comedian and game show host Leslie Crowther.

Ian Anderson (not from Jethro Tull) was the person who first introduced me to Flying Hat Band. Ian worked with World Wide Artistes who managed Black Sabbath, Black Widow and The Edgar Broughton Band. He had spent a great deal of time in the studio with Flying Hat Band producing a 'demo' album. This was one of the best heaviest albums I had ever heard – and today it still remains the best. I believe it was this 'demo' that secured their future. Glenn went to Judas Priest, Andy the bass player to Fairport Convention, and Trevor to the Albion Band. All very successful in their own right. Why the 'demo' was never released I shall never know.

T2 was another three-piece band I became involved with. Pete Dunton their drummer, vocalist and prolific songwriter had already had success with an earlier group Gun, but it was with T2 that he scored highest with an album released on Decca entitled It'll All Work Out in Boomland. This gave the group the recognition they deserved and made several of the music charts. It was highly acclaimed by the critics. They topped the bill at most of the prestige progressive venues and headlined at Earlham Park, Norwich with support bands Free and Hawkwind! Bad Manners supported them at the Mushroom Club in Uxbridge. Although these venues appealed to T2, I much preferred to see them play at the Café des Artistes on the Fulham Road. It was an intimate and informal venue with good acoustics. T2 played their best there in the relaxed ambiance. They never commanded huge fees there, the gig being more important than the fee. It was a gig where their friends and families came along.

There were many interesting encounters during my time with Nucleus and in particular those that took place at the Temple Club. Supertramp were extremely popular long before world recognition came their way, and I always tried to accommodate them at the Temple. They were a great crowd puller and many of the punters who came to see them came in the hope of catching Paul Kossof jamming with them. Paul was liked by all, but his playing varied depending on which planet he was on! He was not always welcome, especially when stoned. Paul had first come to fame in the band Free with the huge, still popular rock anthem, All Right Now.

The son of David Kossof the actor, who played in the TV series The Larkins all those years ago, was a brilliant guitarist and his death brought about by a drugs overdose came as great shock and a sad loss to us all.

Another band that performed well and kept the punters interested throughout their performance was Pete Brown's Piblokto. Because of Pete's songwriting ability, especially those enormous hits he had written for Cream, he and his band always attracted a good crowd. However, Pete had a passion for playing the trumpet and would huff and puff whenever he could get away with it, most of which was ad-lib! Sometimes it worked, sometimes it didn't. His band, always fearing the worst, would spend some time before going on stage hiding Pete's trumpet. These antics seldom worked though and Pete would blow his heart out while his band grimaced behind him. Pete was one of the nicest people I ever had the pleasure to meet in the business. He was understated and sincere. He was one of the 'upper-class' gentlemen of rock, totally in a league of his own. This gentlemanly aura may have had something to do with him living in London's Montague Square.

A lesser-known band that I personally enjoyed was Bubastis. They played a fusion of jazz-rock long before that type of music became more universally accepted. It was always difficult getting them work because of their more avant-garde style, but they were most popular in Paris. They worked there much of the time, never being short of gigs across the channel. The UK was a different ball game. Heavy head-banging being the order of the day.

After the success I had at Nucleus I was invited to work for Acorn Artists on Dean Street. This was more pop group orientated and represented several of the top recording artistes of the day: Love Affair, Christie, Amen Corner, Middle of the Road and The Foundations to name just a few. Again, I had a specific role. This was to promote two UK tours and to help change the image of Status Quo from being a pop group to that of a rock band. Quo went down well at the rock venues I persuaded to take a chance. This they achieved through their sheer hard work. Many venues had perceived Quo as a 'teeny-bop' pop group and unsuitable for a rock venue but the band proved them wrong, going from strength to strength.

On the personal side, I now shared an apartment in Chelsea with Jerry Floyd and actor Stuart Bevan. It was an agreeable arrangement, which gave me the opportunity to delve into Jerry's fabulous import record collection and discover some of the more diverse bands from America. I was also able to obtain some gigs out in the 'sticks' for Jerry. One of these gigs turned out to be a disaster though.

A would-be promoter booked Birmingham Town Hall for a charity benefit. Against my advice, he booked Status Quo and the Equals on the same bill; hardly compatible musically! Jerry was thrown in for good measure and 20 people turned up to see the concert, the promoter having overlooked any form of publicity. Of course, Status Quo fans would have been turned off by the Equals, and any Equals fans turned off by Status Quo. Both bands were poles apart musically. Nevertheless, both bands performed well, that is after they had decided who was going to play first! I returned back to London, not by train that I had wanted to do, but in Quo's Bentley. The learning point for the promoter was, leave it to the professionals. I am sure Quo will never forget that night. It is strange to think that had the promoter only had Status Quo on the bill, and had the gig been publicised, Birmingham Town Hall would have been a sellout!

Thankfully the tours that were arranged for other Acorn agency groups had none of the misgivings of Birmingham and were sold as a package. All the groups on the package complementing each other musically and with full support from their record companies.

Tour number one was a pop tour mainly for town halls, while tour number one was a rock tour for the universities. The pop tour consisted of Christie, Edison Lighthouse, and Worth, while the rock tour consisted of Arrival, Thin Lizzy, and Barrabus. Both of these tours were offered to the promoter for £99 or 60% of the door take, whichever was the greater. However, one promoter, the entertainments secretary at St David's College Lampeter, decided that it would be a good idea to have an all-nighter with all six bands, plus Blonde on Blonde! Blonde on Blonde hailed from Newport, South Wales and were extremely popular at the college. Just for good measure, Flying Hat Band also appeared. They always went down well at St David's. But it was Thin Lizzy who was the toast of St David's that night.

Ted Carrol seemed to have that Midas touch and discovered Thin Lizzy. Hailing from Ireland, dressed in army greatcoat and resembling a farm labourer with his orange beard, Ted helped bring fame to Thin Lizzy, Skid Row and Boomtown Rats.

I accompanied most of the tours when possible. For the Lampeter gig I was determined to travel by train. This I did, enjoying every moment along the meandering South Wales lines. Accommodation was a problem for so many bands and their entourages, with not much chance of sleep. Any spare bed was soon occupied, both in the college and at the local pubs and hotels. The students were most accommodating and no doubt any tutorials that followed the next day would have been poorly attended.

Shepton Mallet was the next venue for the Christie tour and I chose to travel with them. They were fun people and along with Yannie the drummer from Worth all five of us passed a pleasant drive in their Ford Zodiac. Jeff Christie told me about his rise to fame and how he still couldn't believe how successful he had become. It appears that the song Yellow River had been originally written for Brian Poole and the Tremeloes, but they had turned it down. Jeff consequently recorded it himself with two session musicians who later performed as Christie. Jeff was not only shrewd, but one of the most genuine people in the business.

My weekly high adrenalin was often brought down to earth with visits to the parental home. Neither father nor Plum could relate to the life I lived. The only time Plum showed any kind of recognition was when she saw Christie on Bob Monkhouse's Golden Shot programme on the TV. She telephoned all her friends to ask if they had seen Christie on the programme, and how nice Christie were compared to those scruffy Rolling Stone type groups! While father measured any form of success by outward appearances, he actually thought I must have been doing well as I always arrived in a top of the range car. Little did he know that these were contract hire courtesy of Godfrey Davis!

Both tours were highly successful. They would have been even more successful had Prime Minister Ted Heath not introduced a three-day week with power cuts and the like! Ted had already introduced decimalisation, with the cost of living virtually doubling overnight, and he was not at all popular, certainly not in the world of entertainment. He tried to win a few hearts and minds by conducting an orchestra to show his musical skills but Conservatives were regarded as fascists and vultures.

I derived great pleasure from seeing some of the bands play at the venues I had booked them in, especially if I could get there by train. Even better if the train journey was through nice scenery. One band I admired musically was the Pretty Things. I still feel the Pretty Things should have the place of honour taken by the Rolling Stones! But that wasn't to be, although they did have huge success with their albums, S.F. Sorrow and Parachute and several hits in the early 60s. It was a pleasure to have had the opportunity to work with Derek Boultwood and Steve Woolly, who at that time represented the Pretty Things, and thus they played a gig at the Winter Gardens, Weston-super-Mare; a grim seaside town but accessed by a scenic train journey.

The local Musicians Union representative did not welcome their appearance and told them in no uncertain terms that they could not perform, because they were not members of his union! Needless to say, he was jettisoned from the venue. They played superbly as always, and some 30 years later (2004) at Clermont-Ferrand in France it gave me great pleasure to see them still 'bringing the house down'. They looked no different, but played with feeling that only 40 years' experience in the music business can bring. I spoke to their road crew but kept a low profile myself. That episode of my life was over and I am sure that the Pretty Things would not have welcomed a trip down memory lane.

I took great interest in booking one particular venue in Nottingham: The Boat Club. Keith Simons had been the owner for many a year and we both went back to the days of The Crescents. I managed to book some of my favourite groups in there and consequently visit my parents on the same trip. Seeing one of my groups always compensated for a 'home' visit, where I had to endure the cleaning lady, Plum and the plastic covered settee. The latter had never had its cover removed since it was delivered.

I especially recall T2 and Pete Dunton's haunting voice. How one could play drums and sing so well simultaneously I'll never understand. Flying Hat Band with the Black Sabbath type heavy riffs, and Jon Darnborough Bands exciting 'off the wall' fusion of electric violin led rock, are all impressions firmly imprinted on my mind. Jon must have been a sad loss to The Mick Abrahams Band.

All this live entertainment helped make up for the weekend that followed back at my parents' home in Bramcote.

I discovered some years after the fact that during one of those visits to The Boat Club, my future wife had been present in the audience, although at that time we had yet to meet. That was to be some nine years later!

It was during a visit to the Duke of York public house in Yeovil to see Flying Hat Band, after some very successful years in the music business, that I decided to give up the drugs, sex and rock and roll. I'd done it all. Stressed and burnt out, I reflected on what was happening to me and the route I might go if I continued burning the candle at both ends. There had been little time given to personal relationships. Most females only wanted to know you because of what you did, and I had not given any time to my old friends. I had only seen Nigel once during a three-year period and that was at Clouds Club in Derby when he came along for a pint and a chat. He saw and certainly heard Sam Apple Pie. Dressed in drab business suit, he had looked totally out of place among the 'Clouds Club trend-setters'. We tried to talk over the volume created by the band, but to no avail.

When I stood on the platform at Yeovil Pen Mill station, the pangs of nostalgia came flooding back. The beautiful summer morning, the cloudless blue sky, the flowering hanging baskets, the porter's trolley loaded with boxes of Van Heuson shirts awaiting the parcels train, the distant sounds of activity in the signal box – it all alerted my senses. My romantic side had been awakened. That's it, I'm going to go back in the signal boxes! I approached the station porter, and asked if there were any signaling vacancies. "Yes," he said, "but you have to apply through the area manager at Westbury."

I decided that I would do exactly that on my way back to London.

PART THREE

CHAPTER 9

Northolt Junction East and Kensington Olympia South Main Signal Boxes

I left Flying Hat Band in the hands of Ian Anderson and World Wide Artists. I was free. Free of stress, free of commitment. Poorer but happier. I could now sit back, reflect and not be constantly competing. After all, competition was something I avoided back at school on the sports field. It was the reason I discovered what I really wanted, the reason I went my own way; and now I was to re-tread my formative years. To revisit those feelings, emotions, and the romance I held dear all those years earlier.

Okay. So fate had taken me to the GWR. The Great Western Railway (Greasy Wet and Rusty or The Great Way Round) – or now known as the Western Region of British Rail.

View from Kensington South Main looking towards Lillie Bridge. (Author)

Me in Kensington South Main. (David Gould)

Being forever a believer that one's heart should rule one's head, I followed my instinct. From the big money of rock to the secure money of British Rail. These are things I would have to weigh up. Money is the God we English have always worshipped. I had been no exception. Now all this was about to change.

I arrived in Westbury and made my way to the area manager's office. I somehow got past the receptionist from hell and came face to face with the area manager (an acronism from a bygone day) in what appeared to be a museum of GW relics. He gave me a cursory glance when I entered his office, closely followed by a more in-depth scrutiny. Unlike

him, in his BR issue, one size fits all management suit, I had arrived in a brown denim suit etched with pale yellow braid, a tulip collared figure-hugging shirt, platform heeled shoes and hair to the waist. This apparition resembling an Easter egg on legs had actually arrived in his office for a signalman's position! His disbelief at my request was a true picture. But after some explanation and a description of my potted history he began to take my request seriously.

By now I had moved from the apartment in Chelsea and lived in London SW2; I told him that I was prepared to move if necessary. He said

at the signaling school! Back to school? And for signaling? I was beginning to have second thoughts about my second railway career, especially as those in the music business thought I had gone completely off my head. The exception was Pete Way, the bass guitarist with UFO who had the same passion for trains as me.

I caught the Central line underground to West Ruislip passing Park Royal, Greenford East Station, Northolt Junction East, and then after a change from London Transport's Central line on to BR at West Ruislip I continued on to High Wycombe. This was all new territory to me. I did however like the look, the layout and the surroundings of Northolt Junction East. After all, it was the junction for both Marylebone and Paddington and being a junction was interesting operationally.

More trains plied between Northolt Junction East and Marylebone than went between Northolt Junction East and Paddington. The old GW core route out of Paddington to the West Midlands was not a patch on its former self.

Northolt Junction East was a handsome box, still in chocolate and cream livery and constructed entirely of wood. I telephoned the chief and received another blue cardboard ticket to attend an interview at Slough with Eric Voller, the DI (District Inspector), and yet another ticket for a medical in Western Tower, Reading.

I duly past the medical with yet another Scottish doctor and spent the first two weeks with signalman Charlie Britton, who being close on 80 years old, must have been BR's oldest working signalman. He had wonderful tales to tell, was super fit (never wore a top coat) and jumped and ran over the live rails of LT's (London Transport's) Central line on his way to and from work, instead of taking the authorised walking route via South Ruislip station! The only exception to this practice was when Eric Voller was about.

The third week saw me at the signalling school in Western Tower at Reading. I left there as quickly as I had arrived, seeing no point in being there. I knew all the rules and regulations. I did, however, need to learn the Western jargon and their way of doing things. The Western had always done things differently to the rest of BR as England had always done things different to the rest of the world. No recording the bell code in the train register book, but writing in long hand '1740 Paddington' or the 1800 Wycombe! The p-way gangs were called 'Packers'. We had squadron tamping (an engineering term for more than one 'on track' machine) and a 'blocked road' man, a term used for a hand signalman when engineering possessions took place. I quickly learned their way of doing things and subsequently demanded to be passed out on the workings of the box along with the special instructions applicable. This was granted and I took charge on the fourth week.

vacancies existed at Somerton, Bruton and Castle Cary. He hinted very strongly that vacancies also existed along the GW/GC joint line towards High Wycombe. Presumably he thought it better if I was not on his parish! There were vacancies at Park Royal, Northolt Junction East, Gerrards Cross, Beaconsfield and Saunderton. "Wouldn't these be better located for you?" he asked. I agreed and accepted one of the blue cardboard free passes to visit the aforementioned boxes. I was to telephone him and the chief inspector with my decision and they would then arrange a medical! Not another Scottish doctor? If successful I could then start

Northolt Junction East was a spacious box to work and had a pleasant outlook considering its close proximity to the urban sprawl made famous by Sir John Betjeman. It had been well cared for by the signalmen over the years, and although Charlie and I were the only regular signalmen, the relief signalmen on the Western Region all appeared to be well adversed in 'Mary-Anning'. Living in SW London meant my journey to the box involved travelling for an hour on the Victoria and Central lines of London Underground. This worked well on normal weekdays, but became difficult on Monday mornings when it was necessary to be on duty at 0600 instead of changing over at 0700. Sunday night shift being of 12-hour duration with the same signalman returning at 1400 for the late shift.

Northolt Junction East was open continuously and the signalmen changed over at 0700 on weekdays. However, Monday mornings involved taking a BR southern region train from Brixton to London Victoria, a walk across London to Marylebone and then catching the first High Wycombe service to the box. This necessitated getting the train stopped unofficially at Northolt Junction East. Few services stopped at South Ruislip, the nearest station to the box. This practice involved the good nature of the driver and co-operation of the signalman who I was relieving, the signalman keeping the home signal at danger until I had safely alighted from the driver's cab or the guards van.

The high point of working Northolt Junction East was the Paddington expresses, to and from Birmingham and Banbury. The latter being DMUs while the Birmingham expresses were invariably a 'Western' Class diesel. The services to and from Marylebone were predominantly DMUs crammed full of grey-suited commuters.

Northolt Junction East worked to Greenford East Station and West Ruislip on the main lines, while on the Marylebone line to Blind Lane or Sudbury and Harrow Road, but only during the peak hour service. When these latter two boxes were switched through Northolt Junction East worked to Neasden South Junction.

The weekly vacancy list produced a new recruit in the shape of John Widows, a personable chap who arrived one morning for the middle shift, 9-5 (office hours), to learn the 'job' and thus fill the vacancy. John had been a guard at Southall depot and also a guard on LT. He had some wonderful anecdotes and an ability to tell a tale well. He took to signalling like a duck to water and thus Northolt Junction East finally got a full complement of signalmen.

It was feared that we might lose our 'rest day working' by having a full complement of staff, but the concern came to nothing. There were still vacancies at West Ruislip, Denham, Gerrards Cross, Beaconsfield and Saunderton.

Early and late shifts at Northolt Junction East were constant, with the majority of traffic on the Marylebone line. The morning rush hour was 'block and block'. The problem with Northolt Junction East was that signal No. 20 the up Marylebone starting signal was 'free'. The block did not lock it. Therefore, it was possible to clear the signal for a train to proceed towards Marylebone while another train occupied the section.

And there was no failsafe system in place. This unsafe practice remained until the line was re-signalled many years later. The use of a lever collar placed over the signal lever acted as a reminder which physically stopped the signalman from clearing signal No. 20 inadvertently. Northolt was the only box I had come across where the system was flawed. On all passenger lines it was mandatory to have the signal controlling the advance section to be locked whenever there was a train occupying it. How Northolt became an exception I shall never know.

There were many problems with the signalmen at Blind Lane and Sudbury, as these two boxes were for the newest recruits straight off the street. Signalmen were hard to come by and many signalmen employed at those two boxes were not too conversant with English, this not being their first language. Therefore, the signalman at Northolt Junction East needed to be mindful of what might be happening further up the line towards Marylebone. It was very much like working two or three boxes at the same time.

The night shift was reasonably quiet. After the last up and down Marylebone to High Wycombe and Princes Risborough services had cleared, the only interruptions were a Knowle and Dorridge to Dover car train, a Greaves to Northfleet cement train and the Paddington to Bicester Newspaper train. In between these trains it was necessary to stoke up the fire, eat one's supper, put the world to rights on the telephone with the signalmen down the line and of course make your chair as comfortable as possible, sleep being the prime objective. There was, however, another annoying interruption at 0300hrs that was unrelated to the railway. The Meteorological Centre at Bracknell phoned for a weather report! The principal idea of this was for the signalman to give a rough outline of what the temperature and outside conditions were like. Many was the time that these reports were anything but accurate. With hindsight, I suspect that may have been how Michael Fish got his weather forecast wrong on that famous night of the storm.

One evening I met up with Nigel for a pint in the Blue Posts in Soho, followed by a ride in Nigel's Austin-Healey Sprite along the Western Way to Northolt Junction East, where Nigel spent most of the night. Nigel enjoyed working the box and was always eager to operate the levers. In fact, on this occasion too eager! He successfully reversed the Down main home signal to danger in front of the Dover to Knowle

Northolt Junction East Signal Box. A fine example of a GW wooden box. Photo taken from the 1740hrs ex Paddington. (Author)

car train just as it was passing. The driver made an emergency stop and was extremely vociferous!

There was an invisible line between Greenford East Station and Northolt Junction East, somewhere around Pinner, that signified the border between LM and GW. At approximately 0850 on Mondays to Fridays the Greenford East Station block bell would ring one beat 'call attention' in Northolt Junction East box. The signalman at Northolt Junction East would answer only to be acknowledged by the call attention signal from Greenford East Station, him thinking I had called him by mistake, and me thinking likewise!

A telephone conversation followed demanding what was wanted, with the conclusion that it was the 'ghost' who rang the block bell. This went on week after week, until one day there was a strike on the Central Line of London Underground. Now as the Central Line ran parallel to BR all the way past Park Royal, Greenford East Station and Northolt Junction East, we began to wonder why the 'ghost' had not appeared on a strike day. Was the ghost on strike too? After some enquiries with the London Transport signalman at West Ruislip LT signal box we found out that the 'call attention' bell signal was caused by a surge of electrical current every time a set of points were used at Perivale LT Central Line station. These points were only operated on Monday to Fridays at 0850 to facilitate a terminating rush hour tube train crossing from the westbound to the eastbound line.

The Thursday wages run brought the special operating notices and vacancy lists as always. The vacancy lists now covered both LM region and GW region vacancies as traditionally GW vacancies recently transferred under the LM were now advertised on both lists. Kensington South Main box appeared on one such list and this appealed to me. I recalled my first experience there after the night footplate run to Waterloo with Nigel all those years ago. Kensington really appealed to me, so I applied for it and duly received my allocation.

Kensington Olympia on the West London line was under the administration of the Area Manager Kensington. This was a comparatively small area but one of great significance.

Firstly, it was a contingency route for all the four regions of BR. All the four regions could access the West London Line. Secondly, it was the Motorail Terminal for London, and thirdly it was an ideal place for engine changeovers, being situated where no main lines would be delayed. It had direct access to London Underground and had such a configuration of tracks that any train halted there could be passed. There were several routes through Kensington between South Main signal box and North Main signal box thanks to scissor crossovers and facing points located halfway along the extremely long platforms. Many permutations were possible along the four running lines between North Main and South Main. Complicated local instructions existed

regarding the working between North and South Main. These took some mastering, but they were all well thought out, and one could get out of any unforeseen operational dilemma.

Kensington South Main had 75 levers of which most were operational, an array of instruments, and two train describers that no one knew how to work. One was to Latchmere Junction at Clapham, and the other to North Pole Junction near Wormwood Scrubs. These two boxes being the focal points for all routes NSEW.

In spite of these train describers, box-to-box telephone messages for all trains were the order of the day. The signalman, after describing the train with the appropriate bell signal, would then go immediately on the telephone to advise the next box where the train had come from and where it was going. The West London Line was akin to working with the United Nations. Like many London area boxes, English was not often understood fully by many of the immigrant signalmen. There was plenty of misunderstanding, especially when trying to explain which of the three directions a train should go at Latchmere Junction or North Pole Junction. Many West London line signalmen did not have much idea of railway geography. On one occasion, when the signalman at Latchmere asked me where a train was destined for, I had to respond that 'I hadn't a clue', as I had not been informed and was waiting for this information. To my surprise he passed the information on to Clapham Junction as 'Harrow to Crewe' – he consequently received a none too pleasant response from the 'gor-blimey' time-served cockney signalman, and God only knows where that train went!

Kensington was blessed with a supervisor on the platform and a leading railman. The supervisor had made procrastination into an art form, spending much of his time in either North or South Main boxes. If not drinking tea he could be found arranging or interfering with shunting duties of the motorail, or attending to the needs of the passengers travelling on the Anglo-Scottish or West of England sleeper services. Often tugging his forelock in the hope of a tip from some wealthy passenger!

A diesel shunting loco was stationed 24 hours a day at Kensington and when not used on motorail or sleeping car shunting duties would trundle off up the line to Viaduct Junction (just beyond North Main) and shunt the Wood Lane milk tanks at the 'dairy'. Milk trains ran seven days a week across the West London Line to and from Acton, Stewarts Lane, and Clapham Junction. These trains originated from the West Country and took priority.

The life of the signalman at Kensington was one of peaks and troughs. Early and late turns were reasonably quiet. Two morning and evening Kensington to Clapham Junction passenger trains, for the post office workers employed at Kensington, and the daily transfer freight for London Underground depot at Lillie Bridge. There were a few cross London freight trains from Acton to Norwood, Ripple Lane to Hither Green and numerous engine moves between Willesden and Clapham, Acton and Stewarts Lane, and Norwood. Night shift was when all hell let loose with long-distance freights, including my two old friends from Northolt: the Knowle to Dover car train and the Greaves to Northfleet cement train. There were also arrivals and departures of the Anglo Scottish and West of England night motorails and the shunting and re-marshalling of the Stirling to Dover night motorail and its return working. This latter train either picked up or set down the Kensington portion, the night supervisor and the shunter all having their work cut out. How anyone could sleep in their sleeping births while their carriages were shunted and bumped about and re-marshalled I'll never know.

It was on one such night that our newly installed, ex-graduate supervisor Jamie, had to defuse irate Kensington motorail passengers after they discovered that someone had poured white paint from an over bridge on to their cars! The cars were top of the range models and their owners not very sympathetic. I thought it funny. The train looked hideous with its load of white roofed Jaguars, Mercedes and Volvos!

It was one Saturday morning that our station supervisor arrived with about 20 railway-signalling enthusiasts who were all members of an organisation called The Signalling Record Society. I had never heard of this group and was quite surprised that there were sufficient enough interested people to form a dedicated society! Among the visiting party was a wonderfully knowledgeable individual who appeared to have some administration role. This individual was Colin Betts.

At that time Colin lived in Ilford and worked in Whitehall. Both he and I became firm friends, and along with his wife Dorothy, and later with my wife, spent many a happy weekend in each other's company when Colin had retired and moved to Hereford. He was most knowledgeable about railway signalling and life in general. He very much became my mentor over the years. He was the father I never had. His sudden death, outside Hereford signal box in 1988, was a huge loss to the Signalling Record Society, but especially to me. Colin and Dorothy were both the ideal parents. They detested children, but like so many childless couples would have made super parents!

Sundays were the quietest days. From 0900 until 1500 there was no booked service. At 1530 an engine would come from Stewarts Lane heading for Acton Yard to pick up milk tanks from the West of England. Therefore, there was ample time for lunch and a pint or two. It was customary for the North Main signalman and the South Main signalman to meet up halfway along the platform and then toddle off to the pub at the back of Olympia Exhibition Hall. Many were the times that on our return I would find the signalman at Latchmere Junction frustrated by my absence. The Stewarts Lane engine having waited for over an hour for my return! On one occasion I arrived back and immediately received the light engine from Latchmere. After half an hour there was no sign of the engine and when enquiries were made to Latchmere, the signalman reported that he had to fetch the driver and guard out of the pub as the engine failed to move once the signal was cleared. We all liked a pint in those days. My how things have changed!

For reasons I cannot explain now, I had become interested in horse riding. When time permitted, I spent as much time as possible riding across Tooting Bec, Richmond and Wimbledon Commons on hired horses. This was a marked contrast from the smoke-filled venues of the group days. No rock chicks, just eager young girls constantly helping out and grooming horses at the livery stables with a view to a ride on one of the mounts as reward. It was during this period I decided to buy my own horse. That was it. Along with the horse came the expense and the problems. The first being when my horse inadvertently reversed through the window of a fish and chip shop in Streatham! The expense was created by insurance, cost of saddles and bridles etc. I began to ask myself, are the London suburbs really the place for a horse? After all, Streatham and Tulse Hill were fast becoming undesirable areas. Violence and crime were on the increase, traffic was becoming horrendous and I was a country boy at heart, preferring wide-open spaces to the confines of the city and its suburbs.

The answer was close to hand in the form of *Horse and Hound*, this being to the equestrian world what *Modern Railways* is to the rail enthusiast. An advertisement offering stabling, grazing and a country cottage in the Derbyshire Peak District fired my imagination. I responded by telephone from Kensington South Main signal box, went 'sick' the next day, visited Derbyshire and agreed to accept all the terms with a view to moving in the following month.

But what about a future in signaling? After all Trent and Derby power signal boxes had already taken over vast areas of what was once manual signal box domains. How safe would a signal box career be in the wilds of Derbyshire? Anyway, my heart has always ruled my head, and so far I had got by, so let's go for it. Life is not a rehearsal!

I consequently applied for a reduction in grade and to transfer from Kensington to Great Rocks Junction on what was left of the old Midland main line to Manchester through the Peak district. This was granted and I subsequently moved 'up north' and took up the post of signalman at Great Rocks Junction under the jurisdiction of the Area Manager Buxton in the Manchester Division.

CHAPTER 10

Great Rocks Junction and Peak Forest South Signal Boxes

B ags and baggage along with horse were sent north a week in advance of me. I had to work a final week at Kensington. This was a difficult week – had I done the right thing? After all I had enjoyed my years in the 'smoke', but somehow London life was changing for the worse. Violence, or at least the perceived threat of violence, was starting to play an important role. The IRA were becoming very active and on two occasions I was a little too near to their terrorist bombs for comfort. One near Chelsea Barracks and another at Victoria station. One questions one's mortality. This perhaps a little more seriously than the last time I questioned it on the rapid descent to Weymouth on the footplate of Merchant Navy pacific *Aberdeen Commonwealth* hauling the Channel Islands Boat Express.

It was on February 4, 1974, that I boarded an InterCity train at Euston for my voyage of discovery 'up north'. My destination was Chapel-en-le-Frith (South) on the ex LNW (London & North Western) line from Manchester to Buxton. This necessitated a change at Stockport.

On leaving Euston I clearly recall watching the name board at the platform end disappear from view, and thinking to myself, I shall never return! How wrong I was. Little did I know that in later years destiny would take me back and that London would play an even greater role in my life than ever it had done before.

At Stockport I changed from the luxury of InterCity into an ancient DMU at what must have been UK's most dismal station, and rattled along towards Chapel-en-le-Frith. It took forever. We climbed slowly through Middlewood and Disley and on above the snow line to Whaley Bridge. The final assent to Chapel-en-le-Frith was even slower. Snow lay deep alongside the track when I alighted at Chapel. The crisp cold night air hit my lungs. It was pure. The putrid fumes from the DMU only marred

the air that night as it climbed even higher towards Buxton. The diesel fumes quickly dispersed and the train disappeared into Eaves Tunnel. Just the sound of the starting signal returning to danger and the 'train out of section' bell signal (2-1) from the signal box brought a calm that I had long forgotten.

I walked the half-mile up the lane from the station to my new home. It was a full moon and the only sound was my own breathing and the occasional screech from an owl. At last, I was reunited with my horse and belongings. I cried with both relief and emotion. It was to be 25 years later that I would feel the same emotion again and that would be in a different time zone, in a different country. But for now the adventure had really begun.

The following morning, I caught the train to meet 'Bilko' the DI/signaling inspector at the area manager's office on Buxton platform. Bilko only slightly resembled his famous namesake and I always addressed him as Bob, or Mr Keighley. A charming character who always seemed frustrated by the other railway managers he had to work with.

Buxton had certainly been rationalised since the days of steam. It had lost its steam loco shed which had been replaced by four sidings, locally known as the 'Don-a-Roo'. Double junctions had been replaced with single leads, and the double track lines to what was Millers Dale now went to Great Rocks and had become single. The other branch from Buxton that originally went to Ashbourne was now truncated at Briggs Sidings, just beyond Hindlow, and this too had been reduced to a single line. Both these single lines were heavily used for freight and engine movements between the quarries at Great Rocks and Peak Forest, Hindlow and Briggs.

In fact, total line occupation was the order of the day especially between Great Rocks and Buxton. The single line was always congested, as was the diesel depot at Buxton that housed all the locos for

Great Rocks Junction Lever frame and diagram. (Author)

Great Rocks Junction with its flat roof following a fire. (Author)

the quarry traffic plus all the DMUs that worked the passenger service via Stockport to Manchester Piccadilly on the old LNW. The Midland's passenger service via Chinley to Manchester had disappeared many years earlier. It was hard to relate to a footplate run I had on a steam-hauled Gowhole Yard (Chinley) to Buxton freight back in the 60s during a heavy snowstorm. That day single line working was in operation through Dove Holes tunnel between Chinley and Peak Forest, and it took a great deal of time for us to clear the smoke-filled mile-long tunnel at Peak Forest.

Considering Buxton's location in the heart of the Peak District, the freight traffic generated sufficient revenue to pay all the BR staff employed in the Manchester division. I was taken by Bilko in his yellow BR van to Great Rocks Junction and introduced to the most uncommunicative signalman I had ever met. He hated his job, all railway people and no doubt himself. He threatened all people he met with; "You're not coming to my funeral." I doubted whether anyone would have wanted to.

He communicated in a series of grunts or not at all. I decided I should familiarise myself with the

Whoopee! Chapel-en-le-Frith, Dove Holes, Furness Vale, Whaley Bridge, Disley, Norbury Crossing, Hazel Grove and Woodsmoor. All were very easy, straightforward boxes to work.

Whaley Bridge and Hazel Grove both had a 'turn-back' service. They had a 30-minute off peak service which was augmented during the morning and evening by additional commuter services. Furness Vale had gates and Norbury Crossing had the status of just being a level crossing and did not signal the trains, although it did operate signals protecting the crossing. Woodsmoor neither had gates nor even signalled the trains; it just operated wicket gates for pedestrians. It had no indicators announcing that a train was approaching. The wicket gate operator (usually a relief signalman) had to watch both ways for trains, and when he saw one had to lock the wicket gates. This task, or so I was told, was difficult to do from the pub situated a quarter of a mile away on the busy A6 road. Woodsmoor was a soul-destroying place, but had to be open whenever trains ran. Consequently, it was quite a 'money-spinner' and gave me plenty of overtime.

Relief signalmen were also expected to learn signal boxes on the Hope Valley line. Edale, Bamford and Hazel Grove Midland, Grindleford, Earles Sidings, Chinley North Junction, Chinley Station North Junction and New Mills South Junction.

A strange anomaly existed between Peak Forest and Chinley. I was told that the old Down main line became the Up main when the line was severed north of Matlock. This in itself was not difficult for new recruits to understand, but older hands still referred to the Up being the Down and the Down being the Up. One can imagine the confusion. This was highlighted when the new Down line through Dove Holes tunnel was re-laid instead of the new Up line! Evidently, it was alleged that permanent-way records in the home for the bewildered (Rail House Manchester) had never been updated. The end result was that the new Down line that carried the least weight was in perfect condition while the new Up line that carried all the heavy stone traffic was in a somewhat poor state.

I took great interest in the railway geography around the Peak District. Not only was the area still operated by manual signal boxes but among its virtues some magnificent scenery. What finer place to work than Edale or Chapel-en-le-Frith.

The rail network around Manchester and Liverpool was only second to the network around London. In terms of investment, it was the poor relation. It was easy to see where money was spent. There was a definite North-South divide. And even 35 years later little has changed around the Manchester South area.

I took advantage of the promotion possibilities, applied for, and got the post of relief signalman at Buxton.

area and walked the mile along the line to Peak Forest South Signal Box. The signalman, the yard supervisor, and the shunting staff were all more welcoming than 'old misery bollocks' at Great Rocks. I found out that Great Rocks had always attracted signalmen who were a little strange and I made up my mind that I would learn the box as quickly as possible and try for promotion. If I stayed there too long, I might be soon considered stranger than I was already!

There was a vacancy for a relief signalman at Buxton. This covered boxes in the Buxton area.

CHAPTER 11

Buxton Area Relief Signalman

It was while training Whaley Bridge that I first met Graham. He was a relief signalman at Hazel Grove and relieved most of the boxes along the Buxton branch. Our roles overlapped and we often crossed each other's territory. Graham would be at Chapel-en-le-Frith, while I would be at Disley. As 'walking time' was paid from one's 'home' station plus lodging allowance, this oversight by roster clerks could often be quite lucrative. Nobody actually walked to a box. Cycle perhaps, or in my case sometimes by horse!

The days spent in London had adapted me well. Unless someone else was paying or it was to reduce one's tax liability, I did not relish the idea of a car. I certainly didn't need a car in London. If you could not get there by train, bus, cycle or horse, then I was not interested in going. Apart from which, where is the sense of achievement if one goes by car? So it was, that as a relief signalman in Derbyshire all journeys were made by means other than by car.

Cycling was the main mode of transport and although good for my health, did present me with problems during a Derbyshire winter. There was constant drizzle from November to March. It was no pleasant task to cycle from Chapel-en-le-Frith to Hindlow to open the signal box just for a diesel shunter at 0500hrs, when all it did once it had arrived was burble and fart for the first two hours while its driver and guard had breakfast and no doubt did the same.

Hindlow was made worse by the chemical toilet perched precariously on the embankment, which I successfully managed to dislodge while in there. The end result was that the toilet, with me inside it, ended up at the bottom of the embankment – necessitating fresh clothes being brought out by 'Bilko'

Many of the boxes were easy to learn and only took a day or so to do so. All that was necessary was to read the special working instructions. One such box, Dove Holes, situated between Buxton and

Chapel-en-le-Frith was only open for engineering work. All the home comforts had long disappeared and its outlook onto a scrapyard did nothing for its delightful name, which conjured up old manor houses with a dovecot.

The coal fire fumed and smoked, everywhere was damp and rusty and the signals seldom responded to the levers pulled. The points faired little better and required the signal and telegraph engineer to be in attendance whenever the box was open. A night shift at Dove Holes was a sample of what hell night be like. The village and the station were also lacking in charm; if the world had haemorrhoids then they would start in Dove Holes. However, it found its place in the archives when Driver Axon wrestled with the controls of his 8F locomotive as it ran out of control down the gradient from Dove Holes towards Chapel, where it ended up colliding with a proceeding freight in Chapel-en-le-Frith station, demolishing

the old LNW signal box in the process and sending George Howe the signalman on an unexpected rapid voyage from one end of the platform to the other. The present signal box is situated opposite the site of the old one. Sadly, Driver Axon and the guard of the proceeding freight train both perished.

Relief signalmen usually received their 'orders' for the following week on Thursdays; therefore Friday was spent discussing who had paid what to the roster clerk for preferential treatment. This of course was not the case, but more a lack of geographical knowledge on the part of the roster clerk. Or so it was alleged. However, one relief signalman did get more than his fair share of the cream.

It was odd that when I was rostered to relief at Chapel-en-le-Frith I was paid travelling time as if I had come from Buxton, my home station base. I only lived half a mile from the box. Theoretically I had either come on a train or walked from Buxton,

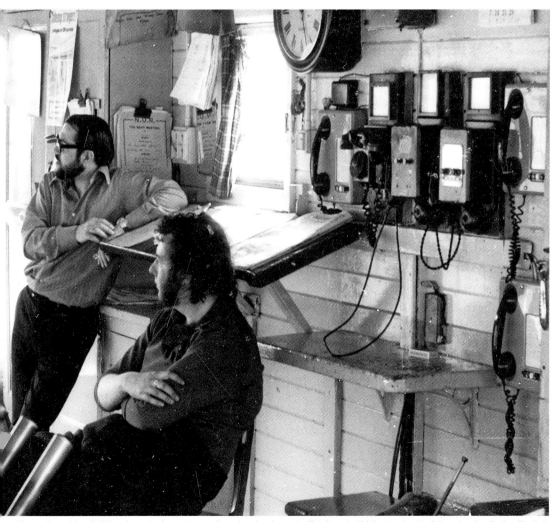

The Author with Relief Signalman Graham Neve, and regular signalman Geoff Ashton in Chinley Station North Junction. (Author's collection)

depending on the time of day. If there was no train service to get you there then you walked. Likewise for the return, unless one was rostered for two or more consecutive days then a lodging allowance was paid! In reality one seldom lodged and the fixed sum paid for this arrangement was inadequate to meet any costs incurred should one have lodged. Nevertheless, it was extremely lucrative. One has to thank the trade unions for this form of unrealistic recompense.

It was one morning while out riding my horse that an unfortunate incident occurred. It appears that my horse was in season and a neighbouring stallion with amorous intentions decided to bolt from his field and mount my mare while I was on her! The end result was a 10-day stay in Stepping Hill Hospital, Stockport and four hours' overtime for the early turn signalman at Great Rocks who I should have relieved at 1400hrs.

In the 70s, BR was considerably more caring than in latter years. In those days they employed welfare officers. Like nurses, welfare officers were born to the job and were very people-orientated. The welfare officer at Rail House Manchester was no exception. He went out of his way to offer guidance and help, along with offers of money to see me over. I was most touched by his generosity, and thought of the difference between the caring society that I was now a part of and the avaricious and uncaring society I had left in the commuter world of London where one never spoke to one's neighbours.

I duly recovered from a collapsed lung, fractured skull and damaged leg, discharging myself from Stepping Hill before I should have done. Stepping Hill hospital was not the place to be ill in!

During my stay at Stepping Hill even Plum, father, Uncle (sorry brother) Bill and Auntie (sister-in-law) Iris came to visit me. This was at great expense said father, who had never pointed the car beyond Matlock. However, they did discover a decent pub, the Waterloo on Taddington Moor. This find helped soften the blow, but not the expense for father. Plum was delighted that father had discovered somewhere different, although he never stopped talking about this new discovery. He did, however, forget the name of the pub shortly afterwards. He used to refer to it as, 'you know the place, up on the moors near Bakewell or was it Buxton?' Bill drove the car back to Bramcote, as father believed that places he did not know were always further than Skegness or Filey.

By now I had integrated well into Derbyshire life and had made many friends. Graham and I shared the same passion for railways and in particular signal boxes. Steve, another signalman, who I had met at Hazel Grove station, before he had joined up to be a signalman made up a trio of enthusiasts for both trains and signal boxes. All three of us were fond of pubs, and in particular their products. We met regularly at pubs along the LNW Stockport to Buxton line, especially Whaley Bridge and Disley.

One evening, having arranged to meet up at Disley I stood waiting for my train on Chapel-en-le-Frith station when a Class 25 diesel loco appeared from Buxton. Something had obviously gone wrong as the engine crossed over to the opposite line and went in the wrong direction towards Whaley Bridge, immediately becoming derailed on the runaway catch points and hurling itself down the embankment! Evidently a passenger train had failed half way between Whaley Bridge and Chapel-en-le-Frith and the Class 25 had been sent out from Buxton to assist.

Not much assistance! The driver and guard were not injured and only complained about spilling their 'brew'. I was then going to be late for my drink with Graham and Steve, and possibly have trouble returning home. I opted for the Good Samaritan course of action and volunteered to implement SLW (single line working) between Whaley Bridge and Chapel-en-le-Frith, using the train I had been waiting for. This I did, having always been a loyal railway servant, believing in keeping the job moving.

I later received a letter of commendation from the 'chief' at Rail House. I also made some overtime, missed my turn of duty the next morning at Disley and consequently received a 'please explain' from the Area Manager Buxton as to why I hadn't turned up at Disley. My non-arrival at Disley had caused much delay and inconvenience for the commuting public. If any lesson was learned from my actions, then it was that old adage: rule one of volunteering – don't.

There was always a sense of achievement when I got to where I was rostered without using a car. However, there were times when I would have preferred to drive, especially when the Peak District vented its wrath.

I have always thought conceptually, although I had never realised this while I worked in Derbyshire; so when confronted with the elements, and a choice of cycling home late at night, or just bending the rules a little, I opted for the latter. Both Furness Vale and Hindlow on late turn offered the opportunity to travel back on the last train, throwing 'Hercules' (my ancient sit up and beg cycle) in the cab or the guards van.

Returning from Hindlow involved riding back in the cab of a 350hp diesel shunter to Buxton and catching the last passenger train to Manchester, alighting at Chapel-en-le-Frith. This was highly irregular, as one should have waited at Hindlow for the diesel shunter to clear Buxton before closing the box. But at least if anything had gone wrong I would have been on the engine. Without the good nature of the regular signalman at Hindlow the following morning, who aided this scam, none of my escapades would have worked. I would have been left to cycle the 12 miles across the moors in the dead of night.

I recall a journey back one night with a notorious Buxton driver renowned for his speed. Class 08

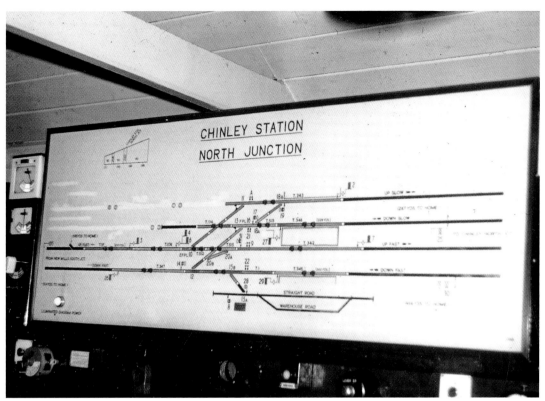

Chinley Station North Junction Signal Box diagram. (Author)

350hp diesel shunting locomotives are restricted to 20mph and one should not let them freewheel down steep gradients! I estimate that 60mph was attained that night just so that I would arrive in time to catch my last train out of Buxton. I can still feel the fear as we crossed the viaducts approaching Buxton.

Another 'slight' irregularity was taking the last Buxton-bound train from Furness Vale back to Chapel-en-le-Frith and waiting in Chapel box for it to clear Buxton. All this went well over several occasions. It entailed great trust from the signalmen at Buxton and Furness Vale. Of course, starting signals had to be passed at danger, otherwise it would have been a shock for the early turn signalman the next day to arrive and find the box not as he would have expected with the starting signal showing 'off'. Sometimes I cycled home, and on a summer evening this was most pleasurable – the road traffic in the 70s late at night being minimal.

Getting to Hindlow for 0500hrs on the early turn was something I had to do on Hercules if I could not swap my turn of duty with another relief signalman. This did not pose too much of a problem as most relief signalmen preferred the early turn, while I preferred the more sedentary after noon or late turn of duty.

Relieving at boxes along the Hope Valley involved great forward planning. This ranged from cycling great distances, walking when it was snowing, horseback to Edale, getting lifts from drivers of freight trains, and getting passenger trains to either drop me off or pick me up at whichever box I was rostered to. Riding on horseback across Rushwarp Edge to Edale for late turn was an exhilarating experience, while the return journey required great trust in the horse as it crossed the moors by moonlight. Earles Sidings box at Hope involved going through Winnets Pass or over Mam Tor. Mam Tor was known for its invisible line that created opposed weather conditions. Bright sunshine on one side and a howling gale on the other side. Mam Tor and Winnets Pass created a vortex and could be very dangerous, especially on Hercules! On one occasion Hercules was blown off the road with me attached! But I always arrived, and was never late. I must have been quite fit.

Grindleford was the furthest outpost and was close on a two-hour bike ride. Although I could catch a local stopping train in one direction that usually corresponded with my rostered turn of duty. Somehow I usually ended up working more night turns at Grindleford than any other. One was never overstretched on nights, but there was always the all-important newspaper train to consider. This train, if delayed, meant that BR had to pay a penalty and therefore it always took priority. Sometimes it

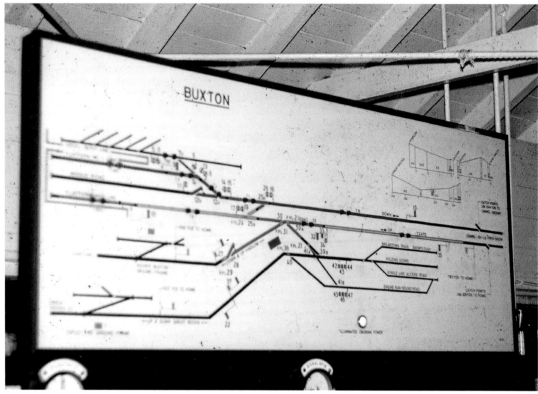

Buxton Signal Box Diagram (Author)

was held back by one of the newspaper companies in Manchester. This happened if a newsworthy story was about to 'break' and it was considered important enough for the train to be held for extra time.

The *Daily Mirror* was the worst offender. This of course did not affect Grindleford a great deal except when single line working was in progress. It was always important that the 'pilotman' to accompany the train through the single line was at the right end of the single line. Many a delay was caused to less important trains thanks to the *Daily Mirror*. The three-mile long Totley Tunnel, at Grindleford, had endless night engineering possessions necessitating single line working and I seemed to get my fair share of pilotman duties at that end of the Hope Valley.

An incident that nearly created a bowel movement was one Sunday evening while I was on 12-hour nights at Grindleford. Most boxes along the Hope Valley were closed on Sunday nights and consequently some extra-long block sections existed. Grindleford working through to Chinley Station North Junction involved a 25 or 30-minute section. In the opposite direction Totley Tunnel East was only about a five-minute section. Therefore, any train immediately following another from Totley would incur a wait of some 20 minutes at Grindleford until the proceeding train had cleared Chinley Station North Junction.

Around 2200hrs the St Pancras to Manchester express passed Grindleford with eight coaches travelling slightly slower than normal. On clearing the section for this train back to Totley I immediately received the empty coaching stock newspaper train. Expecting it to stand at my starting signal for some 20 minutes, I was startled to see it pass the signal at danger and precede six minutes behind the St Pancras to Manchester express! A conversation quickly followed with Geoff the signalman at Chinley. It was suggested that the second train should be stopped at Chinley and the driver challenged as to why he had passed Grindleford's starting signal at danger. With a heavily graded bleak terrain, between me and Geoff, I could only fear the worst as after 30 minutes the St Pancras to Manchester express had not reached Chinley!

Where would we send the emergency services? Had the second train caught up with first? Would we now start filling in the Train Register Book and make the entries relating to the emergency bell code signals that as yet had not been sent? Geoff was always somewhat laid back and not prone to panic and was extremely well composed under the circumstances.

The minutes ticked away slowly. The night sounds took on a menacing air as I scanned the sky towards Chinley hoping not to see anything untoward. I was reminded of horrors past so well recorded in L. T. C.

Rolt's Red for Danger, which depicted in great detail rail accidents of yesteryear. Many of these had taken place on the Settle and Carlisle line, which was not too dissimilar in its terrain to the Hope Valley. Both lines had a similar feeling of remoteness.

After 35 minutes, thankfully the St Pancras came into view and passed Chinley. However, the second train closely followed it! Geoff challenged the driver and it was discovered that he was a little tipsy. He had seen the St Pancras ahead of him in Cowburn tunnel after passing Edale and thankfully had reduced speed. He apologised, sobered up quickly and nothing further was said.

It was agreed that a little altering of timescales was necessary, as was delaying the empty newspaper vans by some 20 minutes at Chinley in order that Manchester Control didn't ask why they had managed to arrive in record time at Manchester Piccadilly!

The same driver returned on the newspaper train some hours late hooting on the locomotive horn 'On Ilkley Moor Bar T'at' to Geoff at Chinley Station and to me at Grindleford. Geoff related this story for some time.

Geoff was a larger-than-life character in more ways than one. He looked like a farm worker who had just had a night sleeping in the hay; his uniform was made for someone other than him; he had a rounded Preston accent that compelled listening, and he held court at the Princes Hotel, Chinley and spent most of his shift on the open circuit telephone. We all 'tuned in' to Geoff when we were on the same shift. Geoff liked a drink and everyone knew this; management turning a blind eye. He was one of life's raconteurs and all the railway men who knew him respected Geoff for his wisdom and humour.

It was early one afternoon when I had finished early turn at Peak Forest that Bilko arrived in the yellow van. He announced that it was necessary for me to go and relieve at Chinley Station North Junction as Geoff had taken ill. The local passenger manager was working the box, and he had little idea of how it all worked.

Bilko dropped me off near to the box. As I approached, I immediately realised something more serious than Geoff just becoming ill on duty had occurred. A police car and ambulance blocked my route, as did a policewoman who demanded who I was and what did I want. Before I could respond the passenger manager appeared in the doorway, somewhat pleased to see me, and explained to the policewoman why I was there. I went in to the box

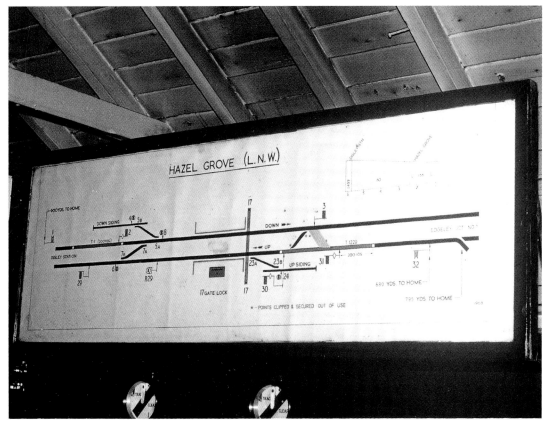

Hazel Grove LNW signal box. (Author)

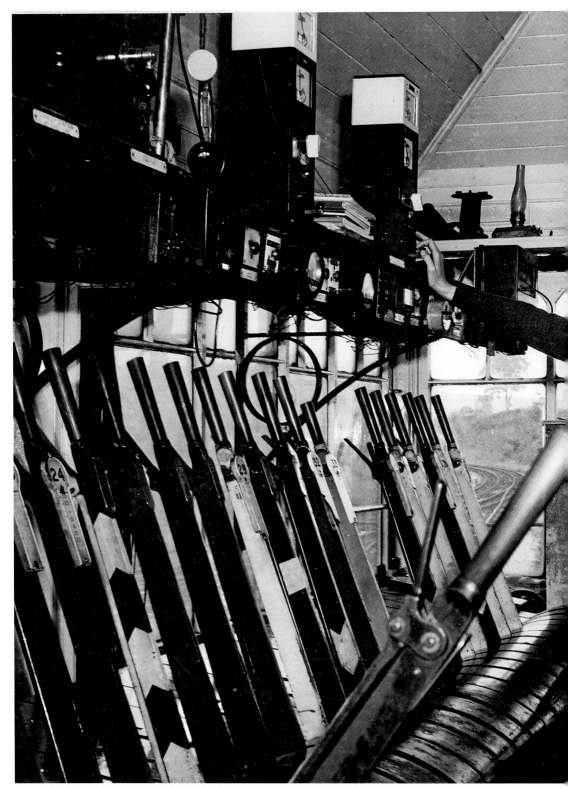

Me working the block instrument to Peak Forest in Chinley North Junction Signal Box. (Colin Betts)

and was horror-stricken. There, lying across the floor, was Geoff. He was dead! He had evidently fallen while cooking his lunch and smashed his head on the stove. I was expected to work the box, stepping over Geoff's body every time to operate the levers or to acknowledge the block instruments and ring the block bells. To make matters even worse, the passenger manager had managed to run through a set of trailing points, making any form of alternative route setting completely impossible. It was two hours before they removed Geoff's body. I never worked Chinley Station North Junction again.

Because of the terrain, the High Peak area was prone not only to adverse weather conditions but also to the laws of 'gravity'. The Buxton area was difficult for all railway operations. Many a daring and dangerous operation was carried out daily at Peak Forest by the railman shunters. This involved the gravitation of 1,000 tons of road stone aggregate from the quarry just to the side of the southern portal of Dove Holes Tunnel. This operation was conducted by hand! One person was responsible for applying the handbrake on several of the leading wagons as they ran down the incline past the signal box. They were meant to come to a stand just before the ground lever frame catch points that protected any vehicle running away on to the main line half way between Peak Forest and Great Rocks. The wagons would then wait for the train engine to arrive from Buxton, while the bank engine would be placed at the rear, to give a helping hand, this gaining access through the ground lever frame. Then the train could depart, receiving a good rear end push from the banker, as it pushed the train up the gradient and joining the main Up line just outside the signal box.

This way it would get a good foothold before it reached Peak Forest Summit just before entering Dove Holes Tunnel. The bank engine would then return to shunting duties at Peak Forest Yard or return to Great Rocks and Tunstead for further banking duties. Meanwhile the 1,000 tons of road stone would proceed on a downhill gradient all the way to Manchester to its final destination at Hope Street near Salford. To me this operation always appeared risky. What if the person responsible for applying the brakes tripped and fell? Where would this 1,000-ton of road stone end up? I didn't have to wait long to find out.

Early one afternoon our 'daredevil' railman-shunter ran the wagons down the gradient faster than he could either run or apply the handbrake! I watched helplessly, but did send the six bells (obstruction danger) to Great Rocks Junction some seconds before the impact! The cloud of dust as some 15 wagons went off the track and careered into each other was akin to a nuclear mushroom! Up and Down main line and the Up goods line between Great Rocks and Peak Forest were blocked for some days.

Barmoor clough tunnel situated between Dove Holes and Chapel-on-le-Frith always received plenty of attention during night shifts for repair work.

The BDVs (breakdown vans) arrived by dusk and commenced the clear-up operation. All went well until the last wagon was rerailed and hauled up to Peak Forest South box by the local bank engine. The coupling snapped and the wagon went careering back to whence it came, scattering the p-way department in its wake. If today's health and safety legislation had been in place then, perhaps the whole of Peak Forest would have been closed down and the staff put in prison! But in those days most 'minor problems' were dealt with locally. After all, no one was injured or killed. It was just another freight train derailment on a non-passenger carrying line.

Because of the steep gradients and heavy trains there was always the chance of a runaway. The section between Peak Forest South and Chinley North Junction through the old Chapel-en-le-Frith (Midland) station was particularly prone to such events. One regular train was the Tunstead (Great Rocks) to Margam. This train reversed at Chinley North Junction. Its route then taking it along the Hope Valley.

To facilitate this change of direction the train proceeded onto the Down slow line at Chinley North Junction stopping with the engine just in front of the Down starting signal. The engine was then uncoupled and went forward to Chinley Station North Junction. There the engine crossed over to the Up slow line to return to Chinley North Junction, crossed over, went back on to the Down slow and then coupled up with its train. When all the brake tests and formalities were complete and a suitable path became available between expresses, the Margam then departed on its journey towards Edale along the Hope Valley. On three occasions the wagons followed the locomotive towards Chinley station depositing a great heap of lime on what had been the old slow lines between Chinley Station North Junction and New Mills South Junction!

On one of these occasions the locomotive returning back to Chinley North Junction passed its own train running away in the opposite direction towards Chinley Station. Failure to 'pin' down brakes and not appreciating the air brake system were the prime causes. It was some years later that the chord line, or the third leg of the triangle was reopened between what had been Chinley South Junction and Chinley East Junction. The reopening of this made the run-round move obsolete and no doubt the good people of Chinley slept easier in their beds at night.

On one occasion, while working early turn at Peak Forest South, I had a hair-raising experience when I managed a ride home to Chapel-en-le-Frith on a Class 40 (40106). The engine had arrived from Buxton to work the Peak Forest-Dewsnap Sidings freight. The engine was in ex-works condition and had been repainted in the old BR green livery. The driver, who was renowned to be a bit of a speed merchant, agreed to give me a lift and we set off with a great roar and a surge of power towards the summit and Dove Holes Tunnel. We entered Dove Holes at 40mph and continued down the gradient at an ever-increasing speed. I reminded the driver that I preferred to alight at Chapel-en-le-Frith in preference to Chinley as our speed went above 60! There was obviously something wrong. Our concerned faces were reflected in the windscreen as we raced through the wet gloom of Dove Holes Tunnel.

The driver's expression was one of strange alarm – so was mine! We emerged from Dove Holes Tunnel went under the LNW Stockport-Buxton line through the short LNW tunnel and continued at an ever-increasing speed through Chapel-en-le-Frith over the main A6 road towards Chinley North Junction. A series of 'pops' on the whistle alerted the signalman at Chinley North Junction of our plight. We were 'a runaway'!

The signals at Chinley North Junction were all at danger, which we passed at a steady 65mph. The signalman was correctly exhibiting his red flag, and we exploded his detonators that had been placed on the rails; these had absolutely no effect whatsoever. Somehow, we managed to slow down and came to a stand at Chinley Station North Junction's Down fast line home signal. I had a long walk back; the guard went off duty with shock and the engine was taken out of service awaiting examination. It remained in Chinley Station goods yard for several days before being towed to Newton Heath depot where its fault was identified as it having had newly fitted defective brake blocks.

It was a snowy Sunday night when I was called out of the Kings Arms to ride the snowplough along the Hope Valley. The idea being that a relief signalman could if necessary open any signal box that might be switched out and thus work points and signals should the snow plough engine get stuck. I joined the two Class 25 diesel locos and their 'passengers' at Chapel-en-le-Frith Midland. The 'passengers' consisted of the area manager, Buxton, a signal and telegraph inspector, and a couple of p-way staff. We reversed at Chinley Station North Junction as Chinley North Junction was closed, and headed off towards Cowburn Tunnel, Edale and east along the Hope Valley. There was little snow on the Chinley side of Cowburn Tunnel as we raced along.

We had a snowplough at either end of the two diesels and were ready for anything. Our area manager had placed his prize 'steam locomotive oil head lamp' on the snowplough as he entered into the spirit of yesteryear! The snow was about 6in above rail height on the Edale side of Cowburn, but we continued our mission albeit at a slightly reduced speed. However, we did not expect to hit a seam of freshly dropped stone ballast that had been left in the middle of the track well above rail height!

The result was a cascade of ballast showering the windscreen of our leading locomotive and severing the brake pipe. We failed between Edale and Earles Sidings, but eventually got under way, I believe, with just a few rules bent. The only casualty was the area manager's prized locomotive oil headlamp. I believe it was never found.

The Government had introduced the 'Threshold Agreement' that was linked to inflation, and each week one received a pay rise. Inflation was really out of control and consequently the weekly pay packet was getting fatter and fatter. We all wondered how long this could continue. But it did for some time and was eventually consolidated into the basic wage. Relief signalmen were now in the money!

To be a relief signalman in one of the most beautiful areas in England gave me a wonderful lifestyle. It was an enviable occupation being next best to being self-employed. There was no boss looking over your shoulder and you made the decisions alone; be it on your own back should something go wrong.

There were times when I did take authority instead of asking for it. The most pronounced was when the Queen and the Duke of Edinbrough came to Hazel Grove as part of her Jubilee tour of England. I had the misfortune of relieving at Hazel Grove on that day, and as the signal box was situated on the platform directly where the royals would disembark, I had a grandstand view of the proceedings. The great and good assembled at the bottom of the box steps to pay homage and to tug their forelock; the Lord Lieutenant, the Lord Mayor, the divisional manager and in the box with me was Bilko. Signal and telegraph staff along with p-way staff all were close by. Police were in abundance and a brass band was playing out of tune. Baskets of flowers along with a fresh coat of paint adorned the station. What an absolute waste of money!

The royal train was signalled from Stockport Edgeley No. 1 Junction long before it was necessary and consequently took ages before it arrived. Bilko became excited and the area manager kept running up and down the box steps asking where the train was. Eventually I received the train entering section from Edgeley and some five minutes later the Class 47 diesel came into view.

The most senior permanent way man was positioned with flag in the exact place where the engine should stop so that the royal party could de-train in line with the red carpet. All went well. The Queen descended to meet the reception committee and I descended to meet the Queen. This was not in the overall plan, but who cared? Strangely enough no one noticed my presence and Queenie toddled off with Phil for no doubt another boring day. Meanwhile, the train had to be disposed of and the service brought back to normal. I often wonder if the Queen realised how much of a problem she caused for the travelling public.

The endless repetition of DMUs on the Stockport Buxton line often became mundane and it was always a pleasure to relieve along the Hope Valley or at Peak Forest. I appreciated the greater variety of traffic. I especially savoured the home-like qualities of the Midland boxes, in particular Peak Forest. It had a resident cat! I never knew whether it should have been called 'Peakie' or 'Forrie'. It was, however, known as Fleabag. I've always loved cats and can well relate to George Bernard-Shaw's quote: "The more I see of animals, the less I like humans." It was with great emotion one dark evening that Fleabag gave birth to four kittens. We all looked after Fleabag and her brood, and when the newborns were old enough, they were packed off into a cardboard box and sent on the lunchtime freight train to Dewsnap. They travelled with the driver and were distributed at boxes along the line. They all survived and the signalmen without exception took it in turn to feed them. The only problem was that they had three meals a day, one from each shift. Consequently, they did become rather portly.

During one of the beer sampling evenings at the Ram's Head at Disley, Steve, Graham and I decided to visit the signal boxes that were still working on the Settle and Carlisle line. The line was under threat of closure due to the expense of maintaining the many tunnels and viaducts. The most costly was Ribblehead viaduct. Our intention was to hire a car at Carlisle and head south, calling in at all the boxes en route. This we succeeded in doing with the exception of Grisburn Ballast Sidings, which we never did find. There was a sense of gloom and resignation among the signalmen, although there was still a considerable amount of traffic using the route. There were a few freight trains and a couple of expresses a day, which ran in the old path of the Thames Clyde Express. These were the only 'takers' for this exposed route across the Pennines.

At Culgaith we stumbled across daytime engineering work and single line working. The pilotman, who was also the district inspector, had landed at the wrong end of the single line with no means of getting back to Appleby where a train was waiting to be allowed on to the single line. We offered, and he accepted, a lift in our car back to Appleby, and consequently we were given the Papal blessing for visiting all the other boxes along the route. We must also have made some impression, as he would welcome any one of us as signalmen on his area should we so desire.

Meanwhile, I had become very interested in the lines around Manchester, especially since Graham had crossed the great divide and gone to the Guide Bridge area and Steve on to the old Cheshire Lines around Altrincham and Northwich. I too thought a change of scenery might do me good, as might promotion, so I applied for a Class 'C' at Edgeley Junction No.1. And, lo and behold I got it.

CHAPTER 12

Edgeley Junction No. 1 Signal Box

A change of scenery is exactly what I got on entering Edgeley Junction No. 1. Firstly, the box was Spartan. Secondly the outlook, unless one admired wasteland and the remnants and decay of the industrial revolution, was grim to say the least. Thirdly, the creature comforts and aesthetic beauty of Midland boxes was non-existent.

The stirrup handled levers; the London and North Western block signalling instruments were all incongruous with the exterior, where 20th century 25kv electric-hauled expresses passed four-aspect colour light signals. All train movements were controlled by 19th century hardware. The only visible contribution to the 20th century was continuous track circuiting. This identified the location and progress of all trains on the illuminated signal box tack diagram.

I got passed out after three weeks and relied yet again on Hercules or local train services to get me to and from Chapel-en-le-Frith. Hercules was usually the last resort as the A6 was not a place to be for cyclists. Going towards Stockport was no problem, being downhill all the way. It was the return trip that was the problem.

On the early and late turns one could witness up to 200 trains a shift, while the night shift was around 80. To help with all of this, some concessions were made. Edgeley Junction had the luxury of a box lad. The term control reporter was not used on what was known as the 'Premier Line!' The box lad was responsible for dissemination of information between boxes and Manchester Control via the telephone, interpreting the tele-printer, and 'skeleton' booking in the TRB (train register book).

Box lads came and went as quickly as football managers. Some worked well, others just took the piss; arriving late on duty or failing to turn up at all. We did have one box lad apprentice foisted upon us during the summer. A graduate on holiday from Newcastle University, he took most of his eight-week stint to master the job, took charge for one week and immediately went back to university.

To identify the route trains should take on the Up line, many additional bell codes were used. It was necessary to know if they were to be routed via Crewe or Macclesfield at Cheadle Junction where the two routes diverged and for us at Edgeley No.1 to be able to identify by the bell code those for the Buxton line. It was also necessary to know if they were either electric-hauled or diesel. There was no electrification towards Buxton, although on one occasion the Manchester to Euston Pullman was signalled up the fast line as a local passenger for Buxton. Thus, the signals were cleared towards Buxton. This caused some delay as the driver actually took the signal and proceeded up the Buxton branch for 50 yards before stopping. This necessitated the train to set back clear of the facing points and created a great deal of explaining to those in the 'home for the bewildered' (Rail House).

The Manchester Pullman was special. It necessitated the station manager at Stockport waving the train away, sporting the all-important bowler hat. A phone call was received at Edgeley No.1 from the station manager if the Pullman departed with any signal aspect other than a green! A double yellow aspect created a storm while a single yellow aspect created a tornado! Of course, due to the density of traffic and the numerous conflicting moves it was not always possible to clear the signals immediately, thus while we at Edgeley No. 1 were exhibiting a red signal because of a conflicting move from the Buxton direction, Edgeley No. 2 was exhibiting a single yellow, while at Stockport No. 1 a double yellow was showing. The station manager had no idea of train movements other than that of his Pullman. Often these station managers at Stockport were newly recruited graduates and seldom appreciated the operations that took place in the Edgeley Boxes. They rarely left the confines of their station, but did have some idea of the discipline procedure and the writing of 'please explain' letters.

I kept in touch through the railway telephone system but seldom saw any of my old comrades. Pinkie was still at Loughborough and Ron was still at Trent, while Bob had turned up as train crew manager at Bristol. Nigel had got married and entered into the world of domesticity; I had not seen him for over a year. The music scene was in the doldrums. Punk was starting to take over from good old rock, with most of it badly recorded. Manchester had had its day as regards decent live venues and was very much in decline. Discos and the cabaret venues serving scampi in a basket had taken over. Second-rate crooners and vulgar comedians all entertained equally vulgar stag and hen parties. Pubs had been renovated by the same pub fitters, all looking the same, selling 'wind assisted lemonade' to an unsavory clientele that necessitated 'bouncers' on their doorsteps. Violence was in the air, and Stockport was no place to be when one had finished late shift at 2200hrs.

I was becoming a little tired of the North West and found the areas around very depressing. Graham, Steve, and my regular workmate Gary at Edgeley No. 2 were my salvation. Somehow the sense of humour that had always been prevalent on the railways in the Southern hemisphere was a little thin on the ground around Manchester. The management was far too task-orientated and not sufficiently people-orientated. Passengers, or customers as they became later, only got in the way of operations. They were overly serious by far. The NUR was an anachronism from the age of the dinosaur and could have come directly from a Catherine Cookson novel! Few people took Jimmy Knapp and his colleges seriously but nevertheless they could upset the applecart when the leadership activated the more militant brain-deads.

Plum and father were becoming older and Plum even more awkward and demanding. She was starting to have problems with father, whose mind was usually somewhere out on the astral. She eagerly wanted to get him in some kind of twilight home. On this subject she was aided and abetted by the 'Daily' who derived a great deal of pleasure by causing as much trouble as possible for the male specie! I believe her husband had left her fairly early on in their marriage; consequently she had a personal vendetta against all males. As Plum felt much the same, they made good allies.

I enjoyed the company of my northern friends, and the excitement of working one of the busiest manually-operated signal boxes on BR, but with personal problems brewing thought it prudent to return to one's routes at Bramcote. This decision was a difficult one. After all, I had reached the zenith of my signalling career; was I going to revert back to a starting grade in the Nottingham Division? Of course I was. As Professor Maslow had intimated in his hierarchy of needs: when one reaches fulfillment in all one wishes to achieve, where else does one go? Usually back to the basic needs, and start all over again. And so I did.

CHAPTER 13

Back on the Nottingham Division. Carlton and Bingham Signal Boxes

By this time the welfare department must have been getting tired of my moves, but nevertheless he pulled the appropriate strings and by mid-November I had back-peddled to the grade of railman under the area manager at Nottingham. Gary helped with the move.

It was an extremely bad idea to return to the parental home. Plum had become very bitter and the Daily was enjoying every minute of my misery there. Father had lost interest in everything except TV, which he watched all day. He was constantly writing and amending hourly on his cigarette packet his

Sunrise at Bingham Signal Box. (Author)

The demolition of Carlton box. (Author)

finances! He still smoked 20 cigarettes a day, never having a day's illness in all of his 84 years.

Both of Plum's dogs would only respond to her or the Daily, and were always given place of honour on the plastic-covered settee. The house had a cold atmosphere and a faint smell of Ellermans Embrication and Dettol. I could no longer relate to my parents. Childhood memories were all becoming hazy. The happy times I had spent as a child with my model railway; Christmases spent watching great aunts scoffing Christmas pudding, while I tried hard to identify their strange aroma; seeking permission, then watching from the loft of their bungalow at Plumtree the Jubilee hauled expresses racing towards Nottingham on the now closed direct line from Melton Mowbray all seemed so unreal and so long ago.

Even the memory of watching from my playroom window at Bramcote for Barton or Trent buses to appear over the hill from the Sherwin Arms on the A52 was becoming almost dreamlike. They say one should never go back as it blots out all too often fond memories; I tend to agree.

The railway memories still hold dear, although when I saw what had happened to Nottingham Victoria and the Meadows area around Arkwright Street I seriously questioned where any progress had been made. This going back saddened me immensely. After all the GC and the GN around Nottingham had been a public service that all of us could tap in to. We could all get about easily without risking life and limb in the motorcar.

A journey made in 1960 from St Pancras to Nottingham Midland behind Jubilee 45565 *Victoria* was achieved in one hour 50 minutes! Try and beat that via Leicester with today's half-sized trains. It makes High Speed Trains (HSTs) pale into insignificance. So, what progress has been achieved?

It was no use trying to adapt to the parental home or their ways. The only course of action was to find an apartment. There were very few decent areas left in Nottingham. It had become an urban sprawl consisting of grim housing estates and fluorescent-lit dual carriageways. The only real decent area left was 'The Park'. The Park was an area consisting of grand houses that had been built at the turn of the century for professional people. The Park was university-owned and had gates at all entrances that could be closed if and when necessary. Anyone who lived within the 'gates' was considered a 'snob'. I became one of them. My small apartment in a cul-de-sac was infinitely better than Bramcote. Although the house at Bramcote had changed little over the years, the A52 had become a noisy six-lane racetrack. Property values had gone down because of this and consequently the area had become more downmarket. Certainly, it was no longer the place for aspiring retailers and golfers with offspring who had attended the school for gentlefolk!

George Hornbuckle was the district inspector at Nottingham. I had first met him many years earlier during an engineering possession at Clay Cross North. George was a gentleman in the truest sense. He was personable, sincere and genuinely interested in you. He had considered my request for a signalling post in the Notts area and kindly arranged for me to fill the vacancy at Carlton and Netherfield on the Nottingham to Newark Castle and Lincoln line. This line, along with the Nottingham Midland to Grantham and Skegness, was still a haven for mechanical signal boxes; Trent PSB (Power Signal Box) having stopped short of Netherfield Junction.

The old Nottingham Victoria to Grantham line, which had run parallel to the Midland line to Netherfield, had closed some years earlier and a new junction had been built at Netherfield Junction, thus allowing Grantham line trains to use the Midland line from Nottingham Midland as far as Netherfield Junction. There, Grantham line trains regained their original route towards Grantham. All traces of the old GN had disappeared under a sea of cheap housing and even cheaper constructed public houses. The only signs of days past were Nottingham Race Course and Colwick Hall, now a pub. There were no signs of the Nottingham Race Course Station or the signal box controlling it: 'The Hall'. Green shabby Nottingham City Transport buses now replaced the steam-hauled non-corridor trains. No longer could one sit on a springy moquette seat and admire the paintings of exciting holiday destinations emblazoned on the carriage wall that British Railways could take you to.

I started training at Carlton. It had Up and Down main line with appropriate signals and controlled level crossing barriers situated between the staggered platforms of Carlton Station. In addition, it supervised an automatic half barrier level crossing at Stoke Lane, between Carlton and Burton Joyce. The latter was just a manned crossing, having lost its signalling status some years earlier. Carlton worked to Lowdham Station in the Newark direction and Netherfield Junction in the Nottingham direction. Netherfield Junction never saw the Newark line trains as the box was situated on the old GN line at Netherfield Junction Station. It was also the fringe box to Trent PSB.

Gary saw Carlton soon after I started to train there and christened it 'A Fish and Chip Shop with Levers!' – I believe he wasn't far wrong as situated immediately at the back of the box was an extremely popular fish and chip shop. Carlton was the simplest box I had ever worked, and especially after Edgeley it was like being employed to do very little. Carlton saw about 20 trains on early and late turn, and two on nights. It was a beginner's box. My ideal.

But first I had to be passed out by the regional operating and area movements inspector (or some similar grandiose title). I will call this person 'The Fonz'. He was dreaded, feared, and disliked by all in the operating and traffic department. He had had a charisma bypass and had an ego like a politician. He resembled a 1956 teddy boy and sported a huge DA haircut, which he perpetually combed, an ill-fitting shiny double-breasted blue serge suit complete with dandruff and stains.

I trained for three weeks and then had to see The Fonz. He asked me two new operating questions. Both had been introduced that day and were published in the weekly notices which were to be distributed along with wages on the following Thursday. I failed the test. I was livid. I was told to come back and see him in three weeks. The signalmen's roster clerk could not believe this had happened and neither could George Hornbuckle.

I telephoned Nigel that night and asked if he knew of any decent pub near to the Park so I could drown my sorrows. He said that decent pubs were a rarity in Nottingham and that one needed to venture out into the countryside to find anything half decent. I told him I was on foot. "Try the Sir John Borlase Warren at Canning Circus," he said, "it has a respectable clientele at 'early doors' and serves a decent pint." Lager, or wind assisted lemonade, was seldom served. This I decided to do.

Nigel was right. The Sir John Borlase Warren was similar in many ways to a London City pub at 5.30pm. Articled clerks, solicitors and lawyers, nurses and doctors from the 'Ropewalk', an area renowned for medical consultants, were all part of the rush and bustle of this most agreeable public house.

It was here that I met Janet. She had just completed purchasing her first house and was having a quiet drink with her friend. I entered into conversation and offered to buy them a drink. I had come out with insufficient money and had to run back to my apartment and raid my piggy bank. I half expected Janet to have gone, but no, she was still there waiting for her drink. We had instant empathy and arranged to meet again. Love at first sight?

We did meet again and I had to sell my father's sovereign ring in order to take her out for a meal, there being a 'cock-up' on the financial front. This was due to me not taking charge at Carlton and thus not receiving the signalman's rate of pay; all thanks to The Fonz. Also, the transfer of all admin from Manchester to Nottingham had gone seriously wrong, as had my change of bank details. Meanwhile there was still the little matter of The Fonz. My signalling chums suggested all manner of devious measures in order that I should get my own back, these ranging from poisoning his tea to, to use a railway term, 'giving his wife one!'

Meanwhile, life at Bramcote was becoming a little daunting. Plum was desperately trying to get father into a 'home'. The milkman knew someone in a very good home near The Forest, just off Gregory Boulevard, so we went to see it. The Indian proprietor was also a doctor. Plum liked that idea. It helped salve her conscience. The home looked clean and the proprietor was amiable enough to convince Plum that this was the place for father. I had my doubts but Plum was adamant. And so father entered the twilight world along with other unwanted folk, and had to be content with aimlessly watching daytime TV with the incontinent and deranged. The only consolation for father, as I could see it, were the teenage nurses who giggled and paraded about the place playing pop music on their Walkmans! Father had always liked a young 'filly' so he would be quite content with the scenery!

I had to endure Plum's choice of TV whenever I went back to Bramcote. This ranged from The Sweeney to Morecambe and Wise and of course Coronation Street. The latter was always discussed with the Daily the next day. "What is Mike Baldwin or Len Fairclough up to?" or "Doesn't Ivy look awful, and what about Stan and Hilda?" Plum loved Coronation Street. I preferred Only Fools and Horses, but Plum thought it downmarket compared to Coronation Street. How she could think that, I'll never know. But then Plum was always difficult to fathom.

Thankfully, all went well with The Fonz and I took charge of Carlton. Regular signalman Eric and I were the only two available to work the box and consequently worked 12 hours, nights and days in rotation. Road traffic was heavier at Carlton than rail, and there was a tendency for motorists to ignore the flashing red lights as the level crossing barriers were dropped for the passage of a train. Many motorists appeared in court after the British Transport Police had conducted a 'purge'. They were usually fined for dangerous driving, but some did lose their licence.

Schoolchildren dared each other to hang on to the barriers as they went up, and one day a schoolgirl, showing-off to her classmates decided to see how far she could go up before letting go. This she did very well, leaving her skirt hooked onto the barrier when she let go and returned to earth. Another instance involved a Jack Russell dog being tied to the barrier on its lead while its owner urinated at the back of the box. I only saw the dog when it was some 15ft in the air! It survived, but always looked nervous when passing over the crossing in the future.

Another tale involved a relief signalman unfamiliar with Carlton who completely forgot to lift the barriers after the passage of a train. He immediately returned to his chair and the newspaper. After sometime he was alerted by shouting outside and realised what he had done. But instead of pressing the button to raise the barriers, shouted to the irate motorist that he was

too near to the barrier and that he had created an electric field force that stopped the mechanism from working. He told him that he would have to reverse about 30ft in order that the barriers could be raised. Evidently it was quite hilarious watching the queue of traffic all reversing back. He eventually lifted the barriers and the leading car driver apologised for being too near! Thankfully The Fonz was not around when these events happened. Which is just as well, as he seemed to lack a little in the sense of humour department.

Early and late turn saw a constant procession of DMUs; the only excitement being the steel trains and oil tank trains. These were hauled by Class 47 diesels while the only express was the Lincoln-Derby mail train. This went through around 2100hrs

Carlton Signal Box a few weeks before closure. The fish and chip shop is directly behind the box. (Author's collection)

towards Derby and woke us all up around 0300hrs on its return. A Class 31 diesel usually hauled this and Nigel often appeared to watch it in the evening after returning from a pub at Thurgarton. He held the mail train in high regard as his father often took him to see it pass Thurgarton when he was a child.

Although Carlton was boring as regards signalling, there was always something to see, always someone to talk to and always someone coming up the box steps for a cup of coffee or a train enquiry. There were railway people who either through poor recruitment policies or some personal malfunction managed to create some humorous interest for us signalmen – their antics giving us endless amusement over the circuit telephone.

One signalman who decided to vacate his box 45 minutes before his shift was over left a message on the level crossing gates for his relief. It read: "Your wages and those of the p-way gang are in the desk draw." And, strangely enough, much to the surprise of his relief, they were still there! This same signalman also painted metal polish on all the windows of Fiskerton Junction box and then wrote 'For Sale' in it. His signalling days were short-lived. His punishment was to be a shunter at Nottingham Midland Station. However, since the closure of the direct line from London via Melton Mowbray, all expresses between Sheffield and London and vice-versa had to reverse at Nottingham.

This involved the locomotive being detached from its train on arrival and being placed at the other end so as to continue its journey. This became rather confusing for our newly appointed ex-signalman as he succeeded in sending a Sheffield to London express back to Sheffield and a London to Sheffield express back to London. He successfully managed to put the wrong engine on to the wrong train when the two expresses arrived simultaneously at adjacent platforms. His railway career was fortunately brief.

I have never been sure whether the characters employed by the railways were made characters by their work or whether they were characters before their employment. Either way, it all made life more colourful.

Bingham Signal Box. (Author)

One early evening while working a 12-hour night shift, due to a vacancy created by a signalman going off 'sick' after to his horse won a race, I was alerted by the local constabulary that I must look out for an escapee from Lowdham Grange. Lowdham Grange was a Borstal institution and the person who had escaped was considered dangerous. Moments after I was informed of this, a youth pressed his face at the signal box window. He was standing on the window-cleaning catwalk. I locked the door, switched off the lights and waited. He eventually went. From then on, I always kept the door locked.

Sadly, the writing was on the wall. Plans were for Netherfield Junction to work through to Lowdham, with the Carlton barriers being operated by CCTV from Netherfield. This meant that I would be dealt with under the redundancy agreement; I could choose another box within my grade and be paid traveling time from Carlton to my new post. I was to make my choice from a 'closed list' of vacancies usually kept for displaced personnel. This included essentially exhausted vacancies that had never been filled, plus a few others from other promotional areas on BR – all of which were under the London Midland Region jurisdiction. It was through these lists one soon became aware of just how big the London Midland region was and what choices one had.

The list I received gave me the choice of: Staythorpe, Fiskerton Junction, Linby and Bingham locally, with plenty more in and around the London Area: Bollo Lane, Kew East, Dudding Hill, and Neasden Midland Junction. These were just a few of the positions on offer. I chose Bingham. Tubs, from Herbert Welch days had lived there and it was on the much-lamented GN and one of the oldest signal boxes on BR. It had been built in 1875 and still retained many of it original features although it had been extended some time after the turn of the century.

It also witnessed the passage of more interesting trains. These included the Harwich Boat Train from Manchester, Toton to Whitemoor freights, Jolly Fisherman seaside specials to Skegness, and a daily Freightliner train to and from Nottingham Freightliner Terminal at Beeston. Petrol tank trains ran from Immingham to Colwick Oil Terminal of Esso and Total. These petrol trains ran via the little-used single line between Newark Northgate, through Cotham and on to Bottesford West Junction. This useful section of railway subsequently closed and the petrol trains had to find another route via Grantham (reversal) and the East Coast main line, or via Nottingham Midland (again reversal) and then via the Midland route to Newark.

During May there was the Spalding Flower Festival. Trains from nearly every corner of the UK came past Bingham with these 'flower people' on board. This naturally caused great problems at Spalding as most of these trains were loco-hauled, consisting of between eight and 10 coaches. Marshalling the rolling stock in the sidings at Spalding must have been a headache for the signalmen. Spalding saw very little activity normally. These 'flower' specials were routed on the seldom-used direct route to Skegness, avoiding Grantham. The direct route ran from Allington Junction to Barkston East Junction, passing under the East Coast main line, while the local stopping service from Nottingham to Skegness was routed via Grantham where a reversal was necessary.

The Spalding Flower Festival was an important event to the new breed of train-spotter who had had the misfortune of missing steam. These new 'diesel' spotters crowded much of the lineside to witness the passage of diesels not normally seen. Rarely seen locomotives from far afield were keenly photographed. There were few passengers but at least BR had the imagination and foresight to run special trains. Merrymaker and Mystery specials were also quite common practice in the halcyon days prior to privatisation. Bingham was very busy on those days and of course Nigel appeared somewhere along the line once he had found out the passing times of each train which had kindly been proffered by yours truly courtesy of the weekly train notices. Picnics in fields adjoining the route were common practice and a carnival atmosphere was often created.

Before starting my training at Bingham, Carlton had to get the seal of approval from the Ministry of Transport regarding the CCTV-operated barriers. Because anything involving the Government takes ages, it was some weeks before I was released from Carlton. Carlton had now become an observation post, overseeing the barriers' function. It was necessary to observe every time they went up or down, and report any defect to Netherfield Junction and the S & T department. This was very boring. Nonetheless, when there was no chance of The Fonz arriving, this observation of the barriers took place from the window of the Fox and Hounds opposite.

Eventually the day came for me to start at Bingham, and immediately afterwards the demolition of Carlton box commenced.

Bingham had a similar feel to it as Kimberley had some 13 years earlier. It operated to Rectory Junction towards Netherfield and Nottingham, and Bottesford West Junction towards Grantham. I succeeded in getting passed out by George Hornbuckle and took charge within a couple of weeks without having to endure The Fonz.

Bingham was a little more interesting operationally than Carlton, insomuch as it had a terminating evening rush-hour train that was badly scheduled just before the Harwich Boat Train. The terminator had to be crossed over at Bingham through points where no signal existed. These points were a long way from the box and one relied on the train crew to ensure all was correct once the signalman had operated them. I always feared this move but all went well. The only incident I had was when I tried backing a Whitemoor-Toton freight train into the Down siding. Either the train was too long or the siding was too short. The end result was an even shorter siding! It was on Control's instruction that I should shunt the train into the siding and I fear they had been mislead by either the train crew regarding the train's length or that the Permanent way had shortened the siding without telling anyone. The latter turned out to be the case. Shortly afterwards the siding was taken out of use permanently.

Father was out with fairies while Plum was enjoying her newfound freedom now that father was in his high-security twilight home. Boscombe and Bournemouth were frequently visited as Plum promised herself she would go there to live once father had 'popped it'. I had succumbed to a car and foolishly agreed to ferry Plum about. The car was purchased from a second-hand car salesman who traded adjacent to the railway line at Carlton. The car seemed okay and a good little runner, although I did have doubts about its purchase after a passer-by told me that I had bought his old car, or at least the front of it! It was evidently a 'ringer'.

Plum flitted from being good-humoured one minute to being vitriolic the next. She was the only person who could raise my hackles. For some reason she had not noticed how Boscombe and Bournemouth had changed since she was younger. Both places had become in great demand by those on the DHSS. Drug-related problems and alcoholism were a major concern. The aging population were having difficulty in living the life they wanted to. This did not deter her from wanting to live there however, since she saw it all through rose-coloured glasses.

By early 1981, Race Riots had started in Nottingham and many of the ethnic districts around the town had become 'no go' areas. Nottingham had deteriorated drastically from the days of trolley buses, and steam trains. Cars had been set fire to. The Park, the Sir John Borlace Warren, Canning Circus and Derby Road all resembled a war zone! Was this where I wanted to live through old age and dotage? After all, I had invariably lived in pleasant areas, and now one had to travel over the county border to find anywhere half decent. However, the ancient county of Rutland had still managed to retain its identity with none of the problems Nottingham was encountering. Derbyshire of course, was still a beautiful place to live, once one got past the drabness of Derby; and, further afield the counties of Norfolk and Suffolk. Were these places to consider? It was time to explore all possibilities and give careful consideration to all the options and reflect.

Meanwhile, weekend breaks to the West Country, Norfolk, the Highlands of Scotland and the Welsh Marches all gave me and my betrothed inspiration. We had to consider our employment. I was happy in the boxes and had no intention of returning to the music business. So in theory, wherever there was a box we could live!

As travel was therapeutic to me, time taken travelling was not the problem it may have been to other people. A compromise was hit. Rutland seemed the best option. Not too far from aging parents, plenty of fairly secure signal boxes, beautiful scenery, good pubs and restaurants with villages of stone, and no more dismal brick housing estates. Okay so Bingham was an hour's car journey from Oakham or Uppingham, but the journey time and inconvenience would surely be outweighed by the quality of life. After all, if one chose the direct route and not the main 'A' roads the journey would be very pleasant.

The decision was made, but all this had to be postponed as two major events took place. Father died and I was to be married. Father had encountered much discomfort in the twilight home, suffering from pain in his hip and back. The doctor in charge of the home refused to admit there was anything wrong with father while Plum showed little concern. I had to take control and call the emergency doctor. Imagine my surprise when the emergency 'on call' doctor turned out to be the proprietor of the home. I ignored this charlatan and called 999 for father's admission to hospital. There it was discovered that he had a broken hip and pelvis! He died shortly after with pneumonia.

We were never a close family but father's death left me feeling as though much of my past had died with him. Plum was nonchalant and on my visit to her shortly after father's death I found her busying herself cutting up father's suits. Suits that he had years before bought from Herbert Welch. She raced from room to room like some whirling dervish, smashing all of his photographs! She had only just found out that he had had a 'fancy woman'. Evidently father had been paying for his 'fancy woman's' dress account, and no doubt other favours. Well-done dad, thought I. Plum thought otherwise, and along with the 'Daily' thought it 'thilthy'. Plum would never admit that the word was 'filthy'. Worse was to follow as it was later discovered that there was little money in the coffers, and that the Bramcote home must be sold.

Plum was now becoming more and more interested in Boscombe and the Dorset coast. It looked like her ambition might be realised sooner rather than later. Meanwhile for me, the evening of father's demise was spent at the Boat Club listening to that most underrated Welsh three-piece group Budgie, consoling myself with Mansfield bitter. I did not feel like entering into conversation with Budgie, and they thankfully didn't recognise me from my Nucleus days. I feel one should not go over old ground. The music business side of me was dead. So was dad.

The music scene was going through a period of change and there were some good bands emerging in the 80s, though they didn't excite quite as much as those of the 60s and 70s. I did like The Associates, Sad Café, Blondie, The Jam, The Police and of course Queen. Ian Dury and the Blockheads, with their album New Boots and Panties, were in my view one of the best outfits to emerge from that epoch.

The Boat Club did manage a few good nights with some heavyweight bands from the 70s. Stray, who were managed by one of the Kray brothers appeared, and so did The Eric Bell band. Eric had been the lead guitarist with Thin Lizzy back in Whisky in the Jar days. It was pure nostalgia. So yet again the music scene was changing and the old wave was giving way to the new wave of punk. Punk was energetic, badly produced, but to some exciting. To me, a cacophony of sound!

I did show my face to one of the bands I had known in my Nucleus days and I did reintroduce myself on that occasion, not at the Boat Club but at Nottingham's Rock City. Rock City had once been a 'scampi in the basket' venue known as the Heart of the Midlands, catering for middle of the road cabaret. It was at Rock City I went back stage to see the members of UFO. They were currently riding high in the charts and had become superstars on both sides of the Atlantic.

The promoter had provided all the goodies as per the 'rider clause' in UFO's contract. A banquet had been laid on back-stage. An enormous champagne buffet took up the length of one wall, while security men stopped anyone trying to enter the back-stage area.

It was nice to see them doing so well, but with their mid-Atlantic accents and their Californian lifestyle they were a world apart from the days of their touring around in an unreliable Ford transit. Their luxury tour bus and pantechnicon were a vast improvement, but no doubt costly. Pete Way was the only member who I could relate to. This was possibly due to him having the same passion for railways as me.

The audience had been getting more and more drunk as the evening progressed. The support band had finished their set, and the crowd was becoming restless. By 11pm the atmosphere was electric and the chants for "UFO, UFO, UFO" were becoming more and more menacing. The time arrived for UFO to make their entrance onto a pitch-black stage and one could feel the tension.

At the first heavy chord from Michael Shenker's guitar the whole stage lit up with enough power to put East Midlands electricity power grid into spasm. The audience went wild and after the first number they were all stamping on the floor in unison for, more, more, more. This did not bode well for the balcony that had been built for the gentile scampi in the basket followers of second-rate cabaret artists. Fearing some breach of security a hurried exit was made, and that was that.

The ghost of rock and pop had finely been put to rest. Or had it?

A small village cottage was purchased in Rutland. It was possible to see the Midland line that runs through the county on its way from Leicester to Peterborough from the back of the cottage. Father would have liked Rutland. There were plenty of aspiring business folk and several golf courses. Plum quite liked Rutland, especially the county town of Oakham, but she was still intent on moving to Dorset. Meanwhile, she opted to stay in a flat in West Bridgford not far away from where my first encounter with steam took place back in 1948 from the comfort of my pram. No London expresses passing now. Only grim new housing estates lurked where once the old direct Midland route via Melton Mowbray to London had existed. An endless procession of cars trying to park occupied most of West Bridgford. What had been a select area just after the war was now regarded as 'bedsitter land' or 'bread and lard island!'

Bingham was 55 minutes from home and although the car was an elderly Audi 80 that thrived on neglect, it needed to be coaxed on a daily basis. It was necessary to have a standby option so a Honda 70 was purchased and on this I travelled daily to and from Bingham, dressed up like a gladiator to protect me from the elements. Even in the height of summer, any speed above 30mph rendered me frozen. Coming home off night duty normally meant that I remained cold for at least two hours after going to bed. But it was enjoyable. Daybreak, the fresh early morning smells before the daily onslaught of pollution, the mist in the Vale of Belvoir, and of course the wildlife all helped make up for the penetrating cold and discomfort.

Bingham was a peaceful box that had little to do other than pass on from Rectory Junction to Bottesford West Junction, and vice versa what it received. Night shift was quiet and I could catch up with sleep after a hectic day.

It was after one hectic day out in the wilds of Rutland that I received a visitation at around midnight, just after 'lights out' and the first signs of sleep. The door burst open and a voice loomed out, "You can't work with the lights off!" I responded with, "I can't sleep with the lights on!"

Yes, it was The Fonz. He had presumably had some marital problem and couldn't sleep and had decided to do a little 'snooping'. He put his signature in the Train Register Book and left. I had difficulty sleeping after that and felt that now The Fonz had discovered my whereabouts there would be little peace and quiet. Quick trips to the Bull for a swift pint while the Chinese takeaway prepared my supper would have to be carefully timed. The extremes of health and safety were beginning to make their presence felt, especially those relating to a swift pint on duty. Of course, rules pertaining to drinking on duty didn't apply to the likes of The Fonz or other managers.

Do as I say, not as I do, springs to mind.

CHAPTER 14

Melton Mowbray Area Relief Signalman

It wasn't long before I went for promotion nearer to home. This was a Class 1 relief signalman position at Melton Mowbray. Melton Mowbray was famed for its pork pies, though most of these seemed to consist of grease, pig-gristle and sawdust. This was encrusted in a cardboard-like shell. They were a delicacy renowned throughout Nottinghamshire thanks to a rather effective marketing campaign. Plum saw them as a real treat, whereas father had always preferred lots of mustard on them to help drown the taste. But then father always used plenty of mustard, as this also helped drown the taste of Plum's cooking.

Melton Mowbray box had control of what was left of the Nottingham to Melton direct main line that was now used as a test track for Derby Research and Development departments. It ran from what was Melton Junction (Ground Frame) to Edwalton. The line was electrified with 25kV and had a speed tolerance of 100mph. At Asfordby, a new colliery had been opened but saw little traffic.

Melton Mowbray box also controlled the goods yard that handled inwards and outwards traffic for Pedigree Pet Foods. In all, Melton was a fairly interesting box with a variety of movements.

The relief signalman at Melton covered boxes at Frisby, Saxby Junction, Whissendine, Ashwell, Langham Junction, Oakham Level Crossing, Manton Junction, Corby North and Luffenham Junction. In addition to the signal boxes there were two manned (or wommaned) level crossings at Wyfordby and Wymondam. Lady crossing keepers, who were constantly at loggerheads with management about the hours they worked and how they could never get any time off work, ran both of these positions and lived in the railway houses provided.

Whissendine was perhaps the most pleasant of all the boxes. It had a panoramic southern aspect across meadows and the rolling hills of Rutland. It also had a ghost by the name of Lou Bailey. Lou was a signalman who had died on duty at 3am some years before. His ghost would manifest itself at 3am in some form or another. This ranged from the wicket gate at the back of the box opening and closing, the sound of footsteps coming up the steps, or the sound of a car at the level crossing. None of these events produced a visual appearance, but did raise the hairs on the back of one's neck.

One signalman did firmly state that he saw Lou standing at the desk leaning over the train register book. It evidently made a lasting impression as he always avoided a night turn of duty if possible and eventually transferred to the next box along the line, Ashwell. I never saw anything but I did hear footsteps crossing the floor. This I couldn't explain, neither could I explain the definite sound of a car waiting at the barriers. On both occasions an eerie atmosphere presented itself.

Saxby Junction, between Melton and Whissendine was only open when required. It wasn't a patch on its former self when it was the junction for the Eastern counties, King's Lynn and beyond. The old M & GN. (Midland and Great Northern Joint Railway), Saxby Junction's 65 levers were then very much in use, compared with the nine working levers since the junction with the M & GN closed in the early 60s.

Saxby Junction was bordering the land of Stapleford Hall, the home of Lord Gretton. Lord Gretton was very much a 'chuffer nutter' insomuch he had his own narrow-gauge railway around his grounds. This was a spectacular affair. It had stations, passing loops, tunnels, and a terminus, as well as a continuous loop around a lake complete with miniature cruiser! Motive power was steam and at certain times he ran the trains for the general public. It was here that a newly built steam locomotive, *Lady of the Isles*, had its first steam trials.

Trent Relief Signalman Ron Cox, Lord Gretton and Me assisting on steaming and clearance trials for Lady of the Isles on Lord Gretton's Stapleford Park Railway, before 'the Lady' went to her new home on the Isle of Mull. (Alan Bowler)

Ron Cox, Alan Bowler (who took the photograph) and myself were witness to this thanks to Lord Gretton. *Lady of the Isles* performed well but had problems with platform clearances. She passed her initial test and was declared fit for service on the Isle of Mull where she was to spend her life. Sadly, soon after, the Gretton estate was sold to the extravert Chicagoan Bob Peyton. Bob was quite a celebrity in the UK and he modelled Stapleford Hall on the English Country House Hotel, demolishing Lord Gretton's entire railway.

Bob's Stapleford Park Country House Hotel and his other outlets in London, Chicago Rib Shack, Windy City, My Kinda Town were huge successes; also his persona was much in demand on TV and radio, where he was often a guest on chat and quiz shows. He was killed in 1994 a road accident on the A1 at Stevenage while returning from London, shortly after his 50th birthday. He would normally have made the journey by train, but Jimmy Knapp had

called a strike and no trains were running! Bob was an aspiring English gentleman who never quite got accepted as a country gentleman. Stapleford went downhill under new ownership, becoming a themed keep-fit type establishment catering for the aspiring 'want-to-be' folk from the suburbs of Nottingham.

I worked Saxby Junction just once during an engineer's possession one Saturday night. It was a cold and drafty box, and the night was made worse by the intrusion of The Fonz. He was now popping up everywhere and had managed to acquire a Fonz 2 along the way. Fonz 2 came from Yorkshire and took an even greater delight in making the life of all operating staff as unpleasant as possible. Fonz 2 was short, fat and uncouth. He was the brunt of most jokes on the signalmen's box-to-box telephone and some good banter took place. He had a tendency to let himself into Saxby Junction box and listen in to what we signalmen were talking about. However, he did learn his lesson when two signalmen either

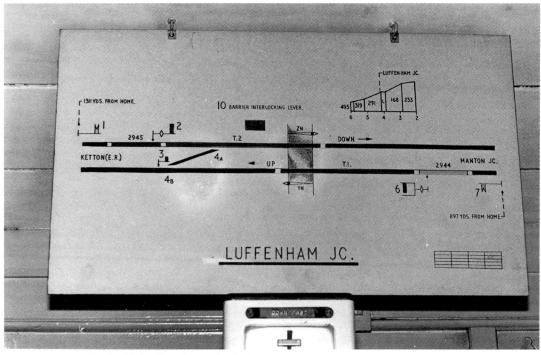

Luffenham Junction (fairly basic) signal box diagram. (Author)

side of Saxby became aware of his presence. They called the police and advised them that there was an intruder in Saxby signal box.

The police arrived and carted Fonz 2 away. Fonz 2 stated who he was and demanded that the police take him to Melton signal box so that the signalman there could confirm his identity. The police did take him there and the signalman denied all knowledge of Fonz 2. That signalman was victimised thereafter.

Fonz 2 was the 'turn up at any time' movements inspector who tested all signalmen on their knowledge of rules and regulations. If you didn't know the answer he would take great delight in making you feel a complete fool, and he prized himself on asking the most unlikely questions.

The signal boxes along the Melton line were fairly easy to work, but often irritating because of all the level crossings. There was always some barrier failure or someone not turning up for duty. With the exception of Melton Mowbray, Saxby Junction and Manton Junction, all the boxes had full-barrier crossings. Beyond the 'frontier' with the Eastern Region at Ketton and on to Peterborough and Norwich, level crossings appeared at about every mile. This was a far cry from the old Great Central where level crossings hardly ever existed. Even little-used farm crossings on the GC had either an over or under bridge. The Midland, however, did not give farmers or even road users such luxury.

I spent most of my days at Whissendine. I enjoyed the peace and tranquility there, which for

most of the time existed. It was Sunday afternoons that caused the greatest problems. With Melton Mowbray closed on Sundays, Whissendine worked through to Frisby. This necessitated Whissendine giving the two lady crossing keepers at Wymondam and Wyfordby authority every time they wanted to use their crossings. There were few trains but endless phone calls. It was difficult to read, wash the car or even worse still to take a little stroll. There was no hostelry nearby and one envied the signalman at Ashwell who could make his way over to the Ashwell Village Club for a quick pint between trains.

It was one Sunday evening when we were all waiting for the last Birmingham-Norwich to appear that we had one hell of a job 'bending' the rules. The Control in Nottingham had advised us that the Birmingham-Norwich was running 60 minutes late and that we would not be able to get a pint. The boxes usually managed to close around 2200 and therefore just make last orders. Well, the news that the signalman at Ashwell might miss his Sunday night pint was more than he could bear. So armed with the news of a 60-minute delay, he promptly toddled off to Ashwell Club. No sooner had he left the box than I received the Birmingham-Norwich from Frisby. Evidently Control had been 'winding us up' and the Birmingham-Norwich was not running late – although it might well be doing if we couldn't get the signalman out of Ashwell Club pretty quickly! No mobile phones in those days.

The express was now approaching me and slowing down as it ran towards the beautiful clear red colour light halfway between Whissendine and Ashwell. Some minutes passed and the driver came on the telephone to enquire what the problem was. I responded that I was having difficulty getting through to Ashwell and if I hadn't cleared the signal in another ten minutes he had better telephone again. Meanwhile, the porter at Oakham had managed to telephone Ashwell Club and alert the signalman. After a 20-minute delay, the train left and eventually cleared Ashwell. Now began the 'coverup'. We managed to falsify timings in the train register book and made it look as though the 20-minute delay had happened on the Eastern Region beyond Ketton. And... we got away with it! However, we all missed out on our pints – though our friend at Ashwell did make it up to us the next time we met up in the pub.

There were plenty of other interruptions from local farmers, police, and of course the p-way and S and T departments. Saturdays often saw the Cottesmore Hunt in full cry, and I would take great delight in telling the master of the hunt that the fox had 'gone away'. The Cottesmore seldom caught a fox and I believe that the fox looked upon us signalmen to deflect the hounds. On one occasion, a huntsman demanded I should stop the trains while they pursued the fox along the railway line. He firmly believed he had the right! How naive some of these people were.

I worked most of the boxes between Melton and Luffenham. I learnt Harringworth and Corby North but never got passed out on the workings. Harringworth was only open for engineering purposes. It had a large scrapyard in what was the old station yard. Disagreeable Alsatian dogs that made it necessary to make a deviation before any entrance to the signal box could be made patrolled this. Corby North was suffering from subsidence and was falling down the embankment. It was also situated in one of the roughest districts in Corby and was frequently vandalized.

Corby had attracted a huge Scottish and Irish immigrant population to work in the steelworks. They enjoyed fighting and following their religious tribal traditions; Catholics and Protestants battled it out regularly at the respective Rangers and Celtic football clubs. I was never in any hurry to take charge of Corby North.

Luffenham proved to be an even quieter box, as it had no part to play in the Corby steel traffic that branched off at Manton, taking the old Midland main line towards Kettering.

The branch line to Seaton and Uppingham closed back in the mid-60s but Luffenham stilled retained the word Junction on its name board. Little evidence of the physical junction existed. Luffenham controlled a full barrier level crossing that was protected by up and down signals. The only excitement was the daily Ketton cement train engine which required shunting from the Down to the Up line annoyingly just as one was making ready the fire etc. for the afternoon shift.

It was this train that one day, on its return from West Bromwich, came sliding past my home signal at danger completely clearing the crossing with the barriers raised while I was unblocking the 'thunder box'. No harm was done and nothing was said. It was fast becoming a cardinal sin for a driver to pass a signal at danger. The term was SPAD (Signal Passed At Danger). There were certainly more cover-ups than ever reports were filed. The signalmen at Luffenham also kept a journal. This recorded unusual events like war breaking out! It also recorded the birth of a baby boy born to a frequent lady visitor to the box. The initials of one of the signalmen penciled in at the side of the entry suggested that this person may have been the father.

Most of my time was spent at Whissendine, Luffenham and the two crossings of Wymondam and Wyfordby. These last two jobs were soul destroying, especially in winter months. After the milkman and postman had crossed the line there was little else to do, except try and tame the rats. Wymondam had a new crossing gate on the Up side of the line thanks to a relief signalman at Whissendine giving the crossing keeper permission to use the road while a train was in section. The relief signalman had a lapse of concentration. The end result was the locomotive hauling the Birmingham-Norwich express arriving at Whissendine with Wymondam's wooden crossing gate emblazoned on the front buffer. The driver thought it hilarious and left the gate for firewood at the box. I am not sure how this was covered up, but nothing of any great importance came of it.

Whissendine attracted more than its fair share of publicity. A new recruit thought it humorous to place an inflatable doll in the signal box window. A policewoman on patrol noticed this doll and was not amused. There was a summons to an enquiry in Leicester for the signalman who on his journey by train from Melton tried his luck with an off-duty policewoman. This was not a very wise move as he was taken out of the box and given the job of ladies and gents toilet attendant on Leicester station. This discipline was no doubt appreciated.

I enjoyed the peaceful life at Luffenham. Nigel's visits were becoming more and more infrequent due to him now married and with 'sprog'. He arrived one evening for a chat. He envied my simple life, with no worries and very little commitment. He was now virtually in charge of the family business and the demands made on him were enormous. He said that he had to earn £2,000 a day to remain solvent! This was in order to meet the wage bill and to keep the business afloat.

I had known Nigel nearly all my life, and although we had seen less of each other over the past year or two, we still managed to meet up once in a while. I was concerned that all was not well. He appeared stressed and worried about business. This was the first time I had seen Nigel so open about his emotions. He usually played any 'emotional' cards close to his chest. Anyway, Nigel had turned up for an adrenalin shot of railway signalling and a trip down memory lane. We talked about the railways of yesteryear, the times we had back in the 60s, and of course his days at Nottingham loco shed. Nigel was convinced that had he stuck to the railways he would be driving HSTs to and from London by now. I pointed out that driving trains now would not give the same sense of achievement as it would

have done in the days of steam. He agreed, and we immediately changed tack to the world of nostalgia and did not dwell on what might have been.

Rumours were rife. Leicester Power Box was creeping towards Loughborough in the north and trying to join up with West Hampstead in the south. Irchester South was currently the fringe box to West Hampstead, but soon the beautiful Midland mechanical boxes at Wellingborough, Kettering, Market Harborough and Leicester would soon be nothing but a memory. I was eager for information as to how and when all this change might affect me.

The railways were going nowhere fast thanks to industrial action, investment was reduced, and to cap it all we had a dictator running the country who had openly said how much she detested rail. I

The haunted Whissendine Box. (Author)

decided that the best way to glean information was to become a member of the LDC (Local Departmental Committee). The LDC was made up of four or five local NUR activists who were paid for time off duty to attend meetings with management and share in a boozy lunch afterwards. This was a revelation to me.

These meetings were generally light-hearted and enjoyable. However, on one occasion all the LDCs from the Leicester and Kettering areas were invited to join regional management at the Grand Hotel in Leicester to hear about the proposed implementation of Leicester Power Box. This meeting was a little heated as some of the LM regional operations management were attending. These people did not suffer fools gladly. They were extremely pompous and looked upon LDC members as complete idiots.

The meeting at one point was adjourned for a quick PNB (piss and nosh break – or personal needs break). We had reached some impasse on a technical point under the transfer and redundancy agreement. I went to the toilet, and from my cubical overheard the next agreed step between the two chairmen. The management said they would agree to a proposal and would set a date to meet again in the future. The NUR chairman was interested in winding up quickly so that he could meet with Jimmy Knapp that evening in Crewe. All was settled in the toilet and the reconvened meeting after the PNB wound up in record time. Nothing was settled. Nothing was signed.

After all was said and done, there was plenty said and little done.

My wife saw an article in the local paper about a 'pig roast' that had taken place in a neighbouring village. She would have liked to have gone to it but neither of us had heard about it. After making enquiries we found that it had been hosted by the local political association. We telephoned their local HQ and were immediately invited to attend their AGM the next evening that was to be held in our local pub. We accepted.

We joined the old retired army major and his blue rinsed, twin-set and pearls wife, listened to the Brian Rix lookalike chairman and before we knew it I had become the treasurer! My wife was a now committee member and it was now down to us to arrange the next 'do'. What had we done? There was no need to worry, as the chairman soon resigned and I became the chairman! Strange as it was, some of our friends also decided to join, mainly because of being able to arrange some exciting village activities – any activities being a little thin on the ground. Politics were totally out of the question. Government ministers were considered complete caricatures and we were not the slightest bit interested in politics, but somehow the events we arranged were very successful.

MPs were, and still are, a necessary evil. Tory heartlands such as Rutland could put up a chimpanzee to be elected for parliament and they would still win. Come the byelection, the Rutland Tory MP won with an increased majority.

The annual dinner for the association attracted most of the county oddballs. Lord and Lady Upshot-Baggerly, Major Dastardly-Minor and his battleship-sized wife, and the retired 'Rupert' who had never lost his 'Prince Charles' accent, that no-one could understand, had all arrived in their best M&S finery. I made the usual speeches, my wife spilled her red wine, twice, over the local councillors and all went remarkably well.

Another event that went well despite the weather was a garden party celebrating the marriage of Sarah Ferguson to Prince Andrew. This was held at the big house in the village belonging to two aged dowagers, Dame Arrabella Wealbrase and the Honorable Victoria Kitoff. They had evidently done something for someone during the war and been recognised for it. We appointed the local silver band to play their 'oompah' music and provided a volatile alcoholic 'punch' called Fergie's Fizz. We provided raffle prizes and a tombola. No one won anything on the tombola due to all the wrong tickets being put in the 'hat'. The Brian Rix lookalike turned up in a pink safari suit and immediately slipped on a wet crazy paving slab with the result that a huge brown skid mark appeared in an embarrassing place, while the village idiot managed to gridlock all the cars in Dame Arrabella's garden. All in all, it was rather enjoyable. Everybody got tipsy including the aged dowagers. We resigned soon afterwards, realising our mistakes. Mistakes must be accepted. However, not to learn from them is not acceptable.

PART FOUR

CHAPTER 15

Promotion into Management

By now Plum had installed herself in a flat next to a fish and chip shop in Mudeford, Dorset. Frequent visits there did little to change my mind that the area was an elephant's graveyard. Lunches in hotel restaurants with elderly blue rinsed ladies suitably camouflaged with perfume to conceal other odours had to be endured monthly. These establishments were usually a nightmare in pink and served wartime food and sweet wine. Even the journey via Waterloo left a lot to be desired, the Southern Region never having any decent rolling stock since the days of steam. No Merchant Navy pacifics hauling luxury Pullman coaches with full silver service, just plastic Formica buffet cars serving at best greasy beef burgers and brown warm water supposedly representing coffee.

The destination was Christchurch. On arrival I was instantly hit by the smell of decay. An aroma of Deep Heat and ammonia seemed to fill the air. The only saving grace for this geriatric seaside resort was the excellent Indian restaurant at Stanpit. It was always a pleasure to head back to the niceties of Rutland. I often returned via Cross Country, thus avoiding the cross London transfer by underground from Waterloo to St Pancras. However, this cross-country route involved encountering Birmingham New Street and the slow and erratic service from there to Oakham. I had that hollow empty feeling in the pit of my stomach whenever I went to Mudeford. This feeling was the same as the one I had whenever school announced we were to play football all those years before. These Plum visits were always difficult. The same conversation every visit, which could just as easily have been carried out on the telephone.

My trips to Mudeford to see Plum were starting to blur happier times in that neck of the woods spent in pursuit of steam with Nigel. I felt that my life was stagnating. A new challenge was necessary. But what?

I didn't have to wait long before my 'motivational button' got pressed. A local 'time served' railway inspector by the name of Reg Jinks is one person who helped change my life the most. It was during a night engineering possession at Luffenham that I first met Reg. He was to act as pilotman during single line working between Ketton and Luffenham. From Monday to Thursday, Reg and I chewed the fat over how things used to be and how things were going to be once the dreaded power box came into force, and also how we would all shape up should privatisation come about.

We scrutinised the vacancy lists. We now had a supplementary list that contained some supervisory posts that wages grade staff could apply for. Reg suggested I should apply for the post of training coordinator at Luton. The specification stated knowledge of the traffic grades and clerical posts in order that one could train and develop young people involved in the Youth Training Scheme.

Maggie had been having problems with high unemployment and it was through the YTS she could massage the figures so it looked as though it was going down. No longer were the young to go on the dole when they left school; they could go straight on to YTS. Shrewd but very effective. Reg convinced me that I should apply but I thought I had about as much chance of getting the job as a snowball's chance of surviving in hell. After all, this training coordinator's job was a Class D supervisory grade – way, way, way up the promotional ladder. After all, I was only a Class 1 relief signalman. Between my lowly grade and a Class D supervisor's post there were seven signalling posts to skip, not to mention supervisory positions A, B and C before we could get to a Class D training coordinator. Anyway, I applied for it on the special application form.

I stated my experience in the pop business, my achievements in management of people in the music business, my LDC interests and last but by no means least my achievements in the Conservative Association. I waited for any response. Nothing happened, so I put the idea out of my mind. Three months later I received a visit from Eric Roberts, the area manager at Leicester, advising me to attend an interview at the regional HQ of the London Midland Region at Stanier House Birmingham. This was to be conducted by a Brian Chambers and a Tim Etherington. Help!

The familiar blue ticket arrived and I caught the train from Oakham to Birmingham New Street. Stanier House was an imposing modern tower block and was the HQ for all the non-operational departments for the London Midland Region: marketing, current affairs, press office, personnel, training and development, administration and of course the general manager, Cyril Bleasdale OBE. All were housed there.

A liveried doorman welcomed me and pointed me towards the reception desk (10ft away). My interview was on the third floor and both Brian and Tim immediately put me at ease. They were very much people orientated and I took an instant liking to them both. Many railway people who had wielded power over me in recent years had been task orientated, and there was a tendency for newly

recruited Fonz types to spring up in the traffic and operating departments. Their inflated egos and condescending manner were akin to those of some junior government minister. Therefore, it was a pleasant change to be treated as a human being and on equal terms.

The interview was more of a chat. We discussed what I had achieved, and then they described the duties of a training coordinator. This was all extremely exciting to me, and appeared to be a huge challenge. I would have no problem training young people in the operating side, as I had trained several signalmen in the past; however, the clerical side of BR was a complete mystery to me, as was the administration necessary to comply with government departments backing YTS.

YOPs (Youth Opportunities Programme) had been the forerunner to YTS and had become a joke throughout the media, with comedians poking fun of what had been perceived as academic failures and 'no-hopers'.

The Government Department was the MSC (Manpower Services Commission) and not the 'Manchester Ship Canal'. Although, as I later found out, this 'Quango' would have been put to better use had it have been used to dredge the Manchester Ship Canal. I returned home in a rush hour DMU

Cyril Bleasdale, director of InterCity – a most humane gentleman. (Alamy)

that lurched its way across the wastelands of the West Midlands. At Leicester it failed and a delay of an hour was incurred before the next eastbound service arrived. I had been feeling quietly confident after my interview, but this delay brought me back down to earth.

I started to think of the logistics I would incur. How would my daily journey work out from Rutland to Luton? The Birmingham to Norwich service was not renowned for its timekeeping and not that many London-bound trains stopped at Luton. Anyway, perhaps I wouldn't get the job, and I was worrying unnecessarily so. The negative 'tape' was playing in my head. Time would tell.

My allocation and joining instructions arrived two weeks later. I was amazed at this huge leap forward. The railways had always promoted people on seniority and never on suitability. But then I had only been used to how things had worked in the past and especially in the signalling grades.

It appeared that suitable applicants took priority over senior applicants in the personnel and management departments of the BRB (British Railways Board) HQ of the London Midland Region at Stanier House. I was soon to learn that the old order of things still existed in the operating HQ of the BRB at Rail House, Crewe, however.

I reported to the YTS training coordinators' establishment at Leicester for my Induction. This was part of the admin block at Leicester diesel depot. It was a grim place, but I soon learnt that the job of training coordinator was not an office-bound job. About 90% of the time was spent at locations on the area. Dave, the training coordinator at Leicester, put the fear of God into me. Terror-stricken is perhaps the best way I can describe my feelings once I realised how much I didn't know and how much I needed to know and do. All of this was new to me.

Luton was to be a new scheme and was to start from scratch, whereas Leicester had been in existence for a couple of years and was established. I soon found out that I would have to acquire an office and all its equipment, a classroom, recruit the first intake, train them in operational and clerical duties, monitor their development, comply with MSC guidelines, and submit weekly returns to the BRB and the MSC.

I would also have to win hearts and minds in all the different functions that were under the jurisdiction of Adrian Shooter, the area manager at St Pancras in order that once the newly recruited trainees had become conversant with the theory of a job, following their classroom training, they could then gain work experience before going on to the next module. The scheme was intended to last two years, with the trainees alternating between 'off the job' (classroom) training and 'on the job' (work experience) training. During the two years' training, the trainees would be exposed to every department

within BR. I was to monitor their progress along with the heads of each department they had work experience with. At the end of the two years they should gain certificates stating their competence. This certification was in its infancy, but if the trainees were successful, they would hold an NVQ (National Vocational Qualification) level 1 and level 2. And with luck BR would have taken them on in a permanent position.

The senior managers at St Pancras were all accommodating and sympathetic to my cause. Adrian Shooter ran a well-motivated workforce. Without exception there was nothing but praise for the boss. Adrian Shooter scored plenty of 'brownie' points by his high-profile style of management. He was always visible to his workforce and never frightened of getting his hands dirty. His enthusiasm for the job was endemic.

The commercial and personnel functions consisted more of 'people persons', whereas the operating or traffic functions tended to be less so. The St Pancras area was a fun place to be and the people there were a pleasure to work with.

One notable person who helped me on my sharp radius learning curve was the commercial and passenger manager Tim Clark. He had a striking resemblance to Noel Edmunds, had a wicked sense of humour and was a great motivator. I was not surprised that in later years, along with Adrian Shooter, they both became bosses of two newly privatised railway companies. Adrian Shooter headed Chiltern Rail, while Tim Clark became boss for Anglia. Fantastic; the right people in the right job. The railways were becoming clogged up with square pegs in round holes during the 80s.

Back at Luton I met the chief booking office clerk, the relief clerk and the staff responsible for the day-to-day running of the booking office, travel centre and telephone enquiry bureau. At St Albans and Bedford, I met the chief clerks and was given their blessing for my sprogs (trainees) to gain work experience at their stations. These included all the intermediate stations between London City Thameslink, St Pancras and Bedford. This major challenge for me to win hearts and minds in this area was a daunting task. I was greatly relieved when I finally had all the support of these people.

I was seldom in the office and while absent the admin side was beginning to build up. Even more so as I had now to win over the traffic departments, signalling and train crew. This was more difficult as there were more health and safety issues to address. Track access had to be considered, what not to touch in a locomotive cab or signal box. Then there was how to conduct oneself with the customers on trains. It was great being able to go as one pleased around the area and to make my own decisions. I reported directly to BRB Regional HQ at Birmingham and seldom had to justify my actions. There was a 'part-time' BR board member who constantly badgered me about increasing my intake of sprogs, but this never came to much, and those at Birmingham treated him with contempt, so I did likewise.

My office and classroom facilities were situated in the old Midland warehouse on Bute Street, adjacent to the branch line that ran from Luton Midland to Dunstable. The line was still active, but only just. One cement train a day ran to the cement terminal hauled by a diesel shunter. This loco was the Luton station pilot and marshalled Vauxhall car trains in the Up side yard and anything else that needed moving. The warehouse had been converted into many different workshops, offices and factories. I inherited three classrooms and an office, complete with a 'steam driven' computer. Only one person on the whole of the St Pancras area knew how it worked. I had absolutely no idea, but was expected to run a computer course for the trainees. At that time, I didn't realise that this computer course was contracted out.

I also found out that I would be expected to take the trainees on a week's residential outdoor development course at the old BRB Eastern Regions Management Training School at Faverdale Hall Darlington. This meant rock-climbing, caving, canoeing, orienteering, problem-solving and decision-making. To assist in all these 'life skills', personal effectiveness tutors were to be appointed to all the YT schemes. These posts were also graded Class D. Where the bloody hell do I start? At least I might be able to get some help from the personal effectiveness tutor, I thought. However, most of these were in need of personal effectiveness tutors themselves. They ranged from 1960s hippies to left wing politically correct females in 'Andy Pandy' dungarees. The trainees ridiculed them all.

Other problems arose. I had to train the clerical trainees in admin and office skills; in booking clerk and travel centre and telephone train enquiry duties; in finance and accountancy; catering and on train commercial duties. The traffic trainees had to be trained in signalling, train crew duties, platform and booking office duties, train announcing, and permanent way duties.

For my part, it was necessary to find the right person on the St Pancras area to undertake the classroom training if I didn't have the knowledge, and to arrange suitable rostering for the trainees to gain practical experience in what they had just learnt in the classroom.

I now had to recruit 18 sprogs. This was mainly achieved through the careers offices in Luton, Bedford and St Albans. The only problem was that many other organisations had already got their own YT schemes and were competing for candidates. These included Royal Mail, Vauxhall and the local council. The careers officers were well intended but failed to deliver, while my own advertisements in the local paper brought very few hopefuls. I eventually started the scheme with 11 people; nine clerical and two traffic trainees.

After their induction week and basic classroom training in admin for the clerical trainees and railman duties for the traffic trainees they were sent away to their work experience locations, while I had to attend a three-week course in 'core training skills' at The Grove in Watford. This was the BRB management training establishment. It resembled a country house hotel, set in magnificent grounds. We had to work from 0900 until usually about 0100hrs. We learned how to write training courses, deliver them and how to use visual aids effectively.

It could have been very easy to become institutionalised at The Grove. The focused rhythm of constant learning with few other topics of conversation was a route to interactive isolation. I now understand fully how recently released university graduates have difficulty communicating effectively once let loose on the grown-up world. Many graduates were at The Grove working on modules associated with the BR management training course with their sights set on 'fame and fortune' in the management hierarchy. Little did I know that at some stage in the future I would be involved in selecting, recruiting, training, developing and assessing their competence! But for now they were pretty unworldly, poor conversationalists, and complete 'piss-heads'.

The principal of The Grove, back at Luton in a classroom situation in a real live training event with the sprogs, conducted my final evaluation. Sorry, not sprogs, 'trainees', as the principal pointed out that I must call them. Political correctness was now raising its ugly head and we were to use a new, unfamiliar, humourless language. I received my 'core trainer skills' diploma with flying colours and was invited back to The Grove to be further developed so that I could become an associate tutor. And to think that only six months earlier I was a relief signalman in Rutland.

The trainees received their NVQ workbooks and immediately drew faces on the pages, making rude drawings of other trainees. The girls, who were the nine trainees in the clerical scheme, were far more mature than the two boy trainees in the traffic scheme. The boys were quite content using felt tip marker pens to join up each other's spots, while the girls did everything in unison – giggling all day at nothing. This job would be fantastic but for the trainees!

I called many meetings in and around the London Division so as to gain suitable work placements for the sprogs. I visited signal boxes on the line from Cricklewood to Acton Wells Junction and enjoyed chats with the signalmen at Dudding Hill, Neasden Midland, Acton Canal Wharf and West Hampstead Power Box. However, I chose the Leicester area for most of the work experience in signalling, placing my two traffic trainees in Wellingborough station signal box – there being far more activity there than at Dudding Hill.

Meetings were becoming more and more frequent. Every function and discipline and every head of them had to be fully aware of what was expected of them. Even the BT (British Transport) Police HQ and the British Railways Property Board were work placements for the clerical trainees, as were freight and passenger guard duties for both the clerical and the traffic trainees. The freight guard duties involved the Bedford local 'trip' freight train that could call at every siding between Bedford and Derby, thus exposing the trainee to a 12-hour shift. Highly irregular but good experience.

The Freightliner train conveying household waste from the London area, that ran from Cricklewood to Forder's Sidings on the Bedford to Bletchley line, was also used to give the trainees experience. The Freightliner involved the trainee riding in the back cab of a Class 47 diesel whereas the Bedford 'tripper' always conveyed a guards van. This often caused great fear for the trainee with its rough riding qualities, especially at high speed. The Bedford to Bletchley line was also used for some signalling experience, although not a great deal happened beyond Forder's. Interesting signalling did exist at places like Ridgemont and Millbrook where the signalling instruments were in the station building and the lever frame outside next to the hand-worked level crossing. Nice in summer, but a fearful job on a wintry rainy day.

Passenger guards duties took the trainees on HSTs to Sheffield and Nottingham. They gained experience on revenue protection, announcing and general customer service duties. They found their varied programme both enjoyable and challenging. Indeed, they had a better insight to rail working than the time-served railwayman who had been in the same job for their entire career.

The only problem the trainees had was returning back to the classroom for the next module of 'off the job' training and getting their NVQ workbooks filled in and signed off by their work placement manager. These workbooks were to be submitted to the City and Guilds in London for final verification and thus if they were to the correct standard, an NVQ certificate would be presented. Sadly, the tabloid media had christened NVQ as 'Not Very Qualified' or 'Not Very Quick'. They had also christened YTS as 'Young, Thick and Stupid'. This did not help recruitment.

BR was very strict about entry examination and education qualifications for YTS. Those who didn't reach the standard were sent the 'Dear John' letter. BR became worried about the initials YTS and changed it to RTS: Railway Training Scheme. This was far more appropriate as the business world had always had high regard for BR-trained individuals. However, RTS eventually got ridiculed too and instead of being referred to as Railway Training Scheme it became 'Really Thick and Stupid'. But then this was not as bad as the Eastern Regions attempt at introducing a team dedicated to resolving failed trains quickly; these were known as Fast Action Response Teams (FARTS).

After the first year's module was complete, the trainees names were submitted to City and Guilds and the MSC and once recorded it was then my responsibility to submit the workbooks. As most of the workbooks bore little resemblance to anything passable, there was little hope of the sprogs receiving any form of certificate whatsoever. Imagine my surprise when one morning I received a large envelope with all the NVQ City and Guilds certificates for my sprogs! No one had asked to see the workbooks, consequently most got ditched and the sprogs carried on with their work placements. They all got jobs on the St Pancras area and it was goodbye to YTS year One.

CHAPTER 16

BRB HQ LMR (Stanier House)

I had now been approached to become involved in two significant projects: the LMST (London Midland Service Training) programme and the Anglo-Danish programme for Network South-East.

LMST was designed for all LM employees to attend. It was championed by the general manager, blessed by the public affairs and press office, and all of those nice people orientated staff at Stanier House, and detested by many of those in the task orientated operating department at Rail House Crewe. The operating department often saw customers as an irritant preventing them from running their Hornby-Dublo. Those who pushed the initiative with great gusto and enthusiasm were those under the charge of the regional public affairs manager, Alan Marshall. He was worth 20 senior managers, and had the ability to motivate all those he came into contact with. He naturally saw the project going some way

Margaret Thatcher resigns. Hooray. A relief to all. (Alamy)

Diana Lamplugh (Suzy Lamplugh's mother). Diana was a charming lady in the true sense of the word. (Alamy)

in reducing the number of customer complaints. These were now at a record level.

To make those who needed to be aware of better customer service, senior managers whose teams interfaced directly with the customer were invited to take part in a little 'jolly'.

This consisted of several road coaches taking the chosen senior managers to a motorway services on the M6, and then leaving them there among the filth and stark surroundings for a considerable time, telling them nothing. After an hour, they were reunited with their coach and taken to the NEC Birmingham for a debrief of their experience. It goes without saying that they were none too happy. Don Mclean, the comedian, was commissioned to act as media host and to find out what their impression of the day was. These senior managers soon realised they had been treated similarly to how BR's passengers, or customers, as they were now being called, were treated. Left among dirt and squalor with no information and no one visible who could answer any questions. Don asked the delegates; "How did it feel?" and "Was it right that people should be treated in such a manner?" not to mention "What should have been done?" and "What could have been done

differently?" Lastly, "What can YOU do on your area to improve the actual and perceived service given to your customers?"

The findings ranged from 'not a lot' to blaming everything except their people, to those who more positive and who claimed they were not aware of the empowerment they were given through lack of training, and to those who said they were perfect and didn't need any further development or training.

It followed that several hand-picked 'trainers' were seconded on to the LMST programme to ensure that all front-line staff were made aware of their customer service duties and what their empowerment was. It was necessary to know when and how to match and exceed customer expectations and thus make life better when things went wrong. 'The train was delayed, but they really looked after me,' would ensure that customer travelled again, and would no doubt tell others how nicely they were treated. It was necessary to remember that one dissatisfied customer will tell 20 others about their dissatisfaction.

To enable all this to happen, it was necessary to have area trainers from the different functions and disciplines assist. The formula was a one-day seminar for 100 staff at Birmingham and 100 staff at Liverpool, exposing them to a discussion type presentation led by Don Maclean interspersed with good and bad examples of customer service situations. These were shared around the room and humorous anecdotes were added by Don. The day finished with the delegates agreeing to meet back the following week in their own workplace, in small groups of ten with their local trainer, and supported by their manager or head of department. These meetings discussed in detail moves that had to be made to improve the service given and ended with firm action plans naming those responsible for implementation.

My role was to recruit some of the trainers and ensure that their facilitation skills were satisfactory. And so, this mammoth project was born.

Running parallel to this on Network South-East was a similar project called 'Anglo-Danish' championed by Chris Green and Julian Drury. It was considered that Danish State Railways and DSB seaways offered the very best in both service and quality. An awareness exchange of staff from Network South-East and DSB took place and best practice was put under the microscope with a view to implementation. I and half a dozen other fortunate trainers were exposed to an intense development programme led by Europe's leading industrial psychologist Dr Valerie Stewart. This covered handling difficult people, defusing conflict, thinking conceptually, making assertiveness work, and handling stress.

These week-long residential programmes helped change my thinking and helped me be more in control of my life.

We were exposed during this period to Diana Lamplugh. Her daughter, Suzy, had disappeared after taking a Mr Kipper on a house viewing while in the employ of a London estate agent. Many ways of defusing conflict and aggression came from these seminars and I am most grateful to both Doctor Valerie Stewart and Diana Lamplugh for the help and encouragement they gave me. Many roleplay scenarios took place that later proved most beneficial when someone on either LMST or Anglo-Danish related some incident they felt could have been handled more effectively.

Both programmes got underway and some 5000 staff went through the training programme over the next 18 months. I claimed squatters' rights in St Pancras chambers, sharing an office with Tim Clarke who was then the area passenger and retail manager. Venues used for LMST were the Adelphi Hotel Liverpool, Birmingham New Street Conference room and a similar 100-capacity venue in Preston.

Suddenly, with only 24 hours' notice, I was told that I was to replace Don Maclean as media host. I did. I busked it, and it went well. Radio microphones, sound engineers, back video projection and a road crew were all a bit like being back in the music business. I loved it. Took to it like a duck to water. It took several hours to come back down to earth after one of these events, much as it had done in the days of The Crescents. I found that I had a natural ability to both train and entertain at the same time. However, my pay never reflected my work, and that I must have been a great deal cheaper than Don Maclean. Although public affairs did manage to wangle me an expensive made-to-measure suit.

The seconded or part-time trainers involved in LMST or Anglo-Danish were expected to volunteer their services when things became disrupted. Special Customer Action Teams (CATS) were formed in every area manager's territory and their role was to aid and assist wherever directed. They would reassure customers, arrange taxis and forward connections, and make phone calls on behalf of any passenger. I too became involved in this and placed myself in some strange roles. One such occasion was during an overhead power supply problem on the East Coast Main Line out of Kings Cross when all northbound West Yorkshire passengers were sent over to St Pancras. Sheffield HSTs were extended to Leeds and East Coast tickets were valid for this purpose.

This was normal contingency procedure. However, I was in the wrong place at the wrong time. Eric Roberts, who was now the St Pancras area manager spotted me on the concourse among the Friday night commuters and advised me that the Duke of Kent and his private detective were expected to travel on the 1600 departure to Leeds. The duke was going 'orff' for a spot of shooting and would I ride 'shotgun' to Derby where the BT Police would

take over? I met the duke and his detective on their arrival and had to arrange safe custody of his guns along with ensuring the two of them a place in first class. This would have been no easy task at the best of times, but on a Friday night with all the additional travellers from Kings Cross, it was near impossible.

It took all of my assertiveness skills to eject two fare-paying first class passengers from their seats so 'his nibs' would not have to stand. I bailed out at Loughborough and endured a horrendous journey back to Rutland. Somehow the railways always fell to pieces on Friday evenings and Monday mornings. I decided that in the future I would use my assertiveness skills to say 'no'.

My Friday night service home was the 1600 departure from St Pancras. It was always 'full and standing' – or to be more positive, 'full and very full'. It was often this train that minor royals and celebrities chose. Princess Margaret and her entourage had to be accommodated one Friday, occupying the entire first class smoker. This was not well received by the first class season ticket holders. I had to battle through the throng to the kitchen to get the G and Ts. The chef, who was anti-royal, took great delight in saying so to all within earshot that he should 'doctor' the G & T's. This did not make my life very easy as BR's on-train ambassador. On another occasion, Omar Sharif travelled on this service and invited all the train to meet him in the buffet for his autograph. Hence, the buffet area was engulfed in a sea of sexually-excited middle-aged northern housewives.

The 1600 from St Pancras managed to become known as the 'Fish'. This came about one evening after the train lurched severely while approached Kettering. About a mile before Kettering there was a right-hand curve that often gave alarm, especially in the galley of the restaurant car. On this occasion, Wally the chef was grilling the fish for high tea when the HST gave a severe lurch and his fish landed on the floor. Wally was not impressed and on arrival in Kettering Station he ran down the platform, opened the cab door of the HST, and hurled the fish into the driver's cab. His words were not for those of a timid disposition. This took place in front of the local press, who were conducting interviews with commuters. Wally became a celebrity and the 1600 became known as the 'Fish'.

A harrowing experience took place on the night of the great storm that caused havoc across the south of England. I had arrived at St Pancras at around 1700 and became immediately aware of things not being right. The concourse was jammed solid with commuters. All silent. The staff had disappeared with the exception of the area manager and Tim Clark, the passenger manager. St Pancras was the only London terminal operating. An emergency or ad-hoc timetable was in operation and only two running lines out of the four were operating. The wind had brought down the overhead cables and

The Clapham disaster December 12, 1988. This helped change health and safety for all of BR and the wider world in general. (Alamy)

HSTs were operating the only services; all electric commuter trains had been put out of service.

Many of the commuters from Wellingborough and Kettering were getting angry. Tim and I did our best at dispatching trains, including some expresses that had arrived from the West Coast Main Line that should have been terminating at Euston. The passengers were counted onto the HSTs at 500 a time. After the first 500 had joined the train, we counted another 500 and then dispatched it.

No signals at St Pancras were working and it was down to Tim and I to verbally instruct the driver to start and pass several signals at danger as far as Kentish Town. The system was working fairly well under the circumstances, but the commuters were running short of patience. One commuter, who believed there was no problem, pushed me off the platform between two Intercity coaches right in front of a British Transport Policeman. He was immediately arrested and lost his season ticket. There is a God!

But the best was yet to come, one morning on the way to my St Pancras office. I was 'making with the teeth' (smiling politely and being extra nice) on a heavily delayed St Pancras bound HST. And, while sorting out a travel problem in the restaurant car, I was told that 'Maggie' had just resigned.

I decided to use this to my advantage, deflecting any anti-BR flack, and announced on the public address to the whole train this snippet of news. Immediately a huge cheer went up that ricocheted throughout the whole of first class. I made the national news that day in a broadcast on 'where were you when you heard about Maggie's resignation?' I got a bollocking for that one, but also a pat on the back for calming down a hostile trainload of commuters with an element of humour. What I shouldn't have said was: 'Here is some bad news and some good news – the bad news is we are running one hour late – the good news is Maggie has just resigned'.

It was December 12, 1988, during day two at one of the 100-delegate conferences at the Adelphi Hotel in Liverpool that Alan Marshall and myself were knocked off balance. Alan was in the middle of his guest speaker's spot, addressing the delegates, when his 'pager' announced there had been a disastrous train crash at Clapham Junction, with many fatalities. It later turned out that some 500 people had been injured, 69 seriously, and that 35 had lost their lives.

This disaster turned what should have been a fun learning day into one of complete gloom and sadness. We all watched the lunchtime news in our rooms while the hotel restaurant waiters twiddled their thumbs. I don't recall anyone eating that lunchtime. Alan went hot foot to the TV and radio studios in Liverpool to quell any fears the public might have of a similar happening on Merseyside. How could it have happened? What went wrong? The subsequent enquiry conducted by Anthony Hidden QC, revealed that it was due to a wiring installation arcing and thus causing a 'wrong-side' failure, resulting in a proceed aspect showing at a signal that was protecting a stationary train ahead. This signal should have remained at danger.

I got through the 'all singing and dancing' and returned home that evening somewhat sadder than when I had arrived. LMST continued for another six months until those non-customer-focused custodians of the finances at Rail House Crewe pulled the plug. Rail House Crewe looked upon 'soft skills' training as expensive; however they never realised that the alternative to not training in this area was to create an ignorant workforce unable to handle people problems! This in turn led to demoralisation and demotivation. Anyway, LMST ended, Anglo-Danish shortly afterwards. In so doing, customer satisfaction on the LM and Network South-East for the first time ever, showed more letters of praise than letters of complaint. In all a successful outcome. But

One stroppy HST driver refused to leave without his PNB (Personal Needs Break) of 20 minutes. I told him he must come with me and announce his intentions on the train's PA system to the 1,000 passengers. He soon changed his mind and left huffing and puffing, chuntering about raising the matter with ASLEF. We eventually got the local 'Bed-Pan' (Bedford-St Pancras) passengers away in an HST calling at all stations and I missed my train home. I spent the night in a hotel that had doubled its tariff because of demand. Market forces, we were told.

what was going to be my next role? After all I had been seconded into a management grade just for those two projects. Was I to return to Luton?

For a short time, I was promoted to Stanier House developing graduate trainees. To help me in this role, I was sent on a further management development course at what must have been the most depressing and dismal training establishment ever: Webb House Crewe. It resembled something from Dickensian times, with food to match. The only thing I gleaned from my week there was that it must have been the 'factory' where The Fonz was made. To this day, I can't remember what the course was all about. I just remember abject misery.

On my return I was then sent back to The Grove at Watford for a further two separate weeks of intensive 'development'. The first week was spent discovering all about stress and the second week a crash course on marketing. A tutor from Lancaster University who was far more entertaining in the bar than in the classroom delivered the marketing course. We learned that many marketing people who failed to think beyond the public's perception of the business advertised made many mistakes. Their products often became the brunt of comedians. Quickfit's slogan 'There's no fitter quicker than a Quickfit fitter' became; 'There's no fucker thicker than a Quickfit fitter' and BR's angry customers when trains failed or things went wrong always repeated 'It's the age of the train', with the emphasis on 'age'.

The most amazing thing I gleaned from the stress course was that few people recognise stress in themselves; it is others who notice it, and then have the devil's own job convincing them they are suffering from it! I soon realised that I had the symptoms of stress and that I needed to change my lifestyle. This was not easy. After all, I invariably achieved a great deal under stress and performed well. On reflection perhaps the less stressful time in my career had been in the signal boxes. Stress in those days being caused by getting to the box!

Music can be a de-stressor, assuming this is of the relaxing type and not of the head-banging variety. My de-stressor was live music at the local pub in Rutland. The landlord had a passion for R & B and engaged many first-rate groups. These groups cost him a fortune, but as it was his first passion, next to brewing real ale, any form of profit-making clearly went out of the window for that one night a month.

Among the 100 or so people who came, I consumed more ale than I should have done and smoked far too many cigarettes. The pub was small and olde worlde. The groups installed themselves in and around the inglenook fireplace and couldn't believe they were to play in such a small venue. I just wished I had had the courage to reform The Crescents. It was a perfect venue for me. Real ale, an appreciative audience all contained in a wonderful atmosphere. No gaming machines, no children, no TV and no mobile phones.

The landlord stipulated that any mobile phone that had been left switched on was to be immediately popped into its owner's pint glass. It was a huge success. The food was excellent also. Sadly, this landlord made it clear that he wanted to retire to France, and was already making plans to turn his dream into reality. I took advantage of his hospitality whenever I could. Finding somewhere this special, I did not broadcast it. There were enough tourists visiting Rutland without attracting any more of the 'kiss me quick' hordes!

Wilbarston village hall was another unlikely venue that had famous groups. There was seldom much publicity and any group appearing there was broadcast through the local grapevine. I missed seeing Wishbone Ash, but did manage to see Albert Lee, Mike Berry and Hogan's Heroes, with Pete Winfield on piano. I had first seen Albert Lee way back at the Temple Club when he fronted Heads Hands and Feet. Albert was the uncrowned king of rock and country guitar but seemed to take a low profile. I had also seen him in concert at the theatre in Melton Mowbray when I had been a relief signalman there. He had always impressed me with his playing, especially on Country Boy. It was many years later that I saw him play on the 'Stratpack' concert at Wembley with all the superstars associated with the Fender Stratocaster guitar. He performed with The Crickets, Brian May and Ronnie Wood. He also played Country Boy accompanied by Theresa Anderson on violin. Excellent. Albert's guitar playing always makes me want to give up my guitar. Now that would have pleased Plum!

Rail House Crewe (the home for the bewildered). (Alamy)

Following my return to civilization at Stanier House away from the academic world of The Grove, my role was to obtain release for eight graduates from their place of work around the country and write a training event for them on 'presentation skills'. I was to advise the MS4 (everyone referred to each other by grade) next week when I had managed the release of these trainees. I advised him later that day. He was shocked that I had done this so quickly and suggested that this task was usually spread over a week! He suggested I should do what plenty of others do, which was to walk slowly from basement to top floor canteen, have lunch and return to the basement in time for going home. Talk to everyone and always carry some papers with you. So that was how senior management spent their time.

I ran the presentation course for the eight graduates at a four-star hotel in Birmingham and found them nice but dim. They were slow to respond and unwilling to accept feedback. Their brief was to make a presentation using visual aids effectively and to contain this to a maximum of 30 minutes' duration. I spent the daytime delivering classroom input on hints, skills and tips, and the evening spent assisting them in preparation for their presentation. I decided that as their railway knowledge was zero, it would be better for them to choose their own presentation topic. These varied from stamp collecting to flower arranging. One extremely delicate female, who jumped out of her skin every time someone spoke to her, chose as her presentation The Life of Pre-Raphaelite Women.

I found it interesting to glean from graduate trainees where they wanted their first management appointment to be. The appointment was never where they wanted, as BR thought that it good for character building if one was appointed somewhere where problems would occur and a long way away from home. Sadistic bastards really!

My daily journey from Rutland to New Street and back in an uncomfortable DMU in the depths of winter was no way to pass time. My so-called senior management role was basic and elementary and I derived little satisfaction out of being cooped up in Stanier House. Although I learned a great deal in how the hierarchy worked at senior level, I never actually learnt what people did. HQ staff talked in riddles. They referred to people by their grade. 'Oh, you know, he's the MS3 in marketing' or 'she was a CO2 in the travel centre but she got the CO4's job'. This was like pigeonholing people into their socio-economic group or trying to assess their bank balance. I always took great delight in asking people to tell me what they did as opposed to what their grade was.

The daily grind to Brum left little time for friends and family as one was expected to turn up at 8.45 and not leave the premises until late afternoon, which always seemed too late to catch my train home.

Working (or attending) 14 hours a day became the norm. It seemed strange to me that in the computer age we all went off to an office to do the work we could do at home.

My world changed as quickly into positive mode as it had into negative. I was asked to become involved in senior conductor training for InterCity. Guards were to have a completely new title and job description and were to be retrained in their roles and responsibilities. Courses were to be residential and last five days. Because of their new high profile customer service role, quality three- and four-star hotels were chosen. This sounds better than walking around Stanier House, thought I.

InterCity had rewritten the job descriptions of guards and their new high profile, up front, customer focused image along with new uniforms was soon to go 'live'.

Twelve InterCity guards spent five days each week in hotels where excellent customer service was the norm. They learnt all about what was expected of them. They were taught how and when to use authority, how to handle conflict, to know the parameters of their empowerment, to understand body language and to know when and how to match and exceed customer expectations. They were taught proactive measures that would enable quick repairs to their train sets once the train was back at its depot, and they visited the InterCity depots to appreciate the problems encountered by the maintenance teams. These depots were Craigentinney (Edinburgh), Bounds Green, Wembley, Oxley (Wolverhampton), Longsight (Manchester), Neville Hill (Leeds) and Etches Park (Derby). All InterCity guards on the West Coast Main Line, Midland Main Line and InterCity Cross Country went through this programme. The Eastern Region and Great Western Region followed some months after. The London Midland prided itself in being the innovators, and the West Coast Main Line out of London Euston still regarded itself as the Premier Line.

The training courses ran for about six months. I was accompanied on these courses by the local guards inspector who helped with the technical issues and the old 'stick in the mud'. It came as no surprise that the negative 'Nellies' were mainly based at Crewe. This I feared was the result of years of authoritarian-style management. There was a real 'us and them' attitude problem at Crewe that had never been addressed. This had manifested itself throughout the front-line staff. Second and third generation railmen inherited this attitude.

Customers were seen as a 'pain in the arse'. The fact that some customers may well have been awkward, arrogant, self-opinionated and condescending was perhaps correct, but at the end of the day one has to accept the customer is always right. Without them 'you ain't got a job matey'. The 'customer is always right' policy was a difficult one for the Crewe frontline staff to accept.

An interesting interlude happened during a tour of the West Coast Main Line to familiarise myself with InterCity depots. I had stopped off at one mainline station and got into conversation with a booking clerk who bemoaned the fact that he got all the aggressive and awkward customers, while the young lady at the next window had an easy time and could spend all day polishing her nails. He had come to the conclusion that as he was the first booking clerk they saw, this was the reason he got all the problems. I suggested he swapped places with the young lady. This he did, and he still said he had all the problems and aggressive people; they still found him, while she still sat there polishing her nails! I was determined to find out what the problem was.

I simply asked, "How do you treat people?" He said: "I treat people how they treat me." And that, was the problem! If the customer was rude, he was rude back and then things just escalated. Presumably, someone not dissimilar from him had trained him in the job, and not in handling the customer. He was a result of poor recruitment and no training and development in interpersonal skills. There were plenty like him on BR. Things would have to change when privatisation came about and people could make a choice in how they travelled.

Competition was a new issue. People like our booking clerk never realised that customers had a choice as to how they spent their money. Their view of competition was that of plane, bus or taxi. They didn't think that people might choose to spend their money on decorating the bedroom or having an Indian meal, instead of having a day out somewhere, using the train to get there.

On another tour of the network getting to know the routes, depots and behind the scenes operations, I encountered a wonderful interaction between a Fonz-type senior manager and a supervisor at Crewe. The Fonz came out with the classic: "Do you know who I am?" and got the magnificent response of: "If you can remember where you live we'll get you home, and there may be someone there who knows who you are." Why can't I come out with these immediate put-downs? The Fonz could not believe that a member of staff could speak to him in that manner. Not for one moment did he think that it was a very clever response to his arrogant and condescending manner. The supervisor quickly got nominated for a customer service training course, whereas it was the Fonz who needed the course. But like many of the senior managers, they firmly believed they were above all of that.

For the senior conductor training, real letters of complaint supplied by the public affairs office in Birmingham were used as a basis for debate and discussion. Many roleplay scenarios coming from this source turned out to be extremely beneficial to the delegates; many wished they had been trained in these people skills at the time of their induction. I was able to carry out these professionally thanks to my earlier training and development with Doctor Valerie Stewart.

Classroom training took up most of the day for the first part of the week. This involved familiarising guards with their new role as senior conductor, assistance being given by their manager. Then by the second half of the week they were developing the interpersonal skills required to be more effective. The evenings were spent practicing voice skills and discussing real life dramas that had happened to customers on InterCity trains. Finally, they were taken to an InterCity depot at night to see what happens to their 'fault' reports and what occurs to their train sets. Open discussion with foremen and fitters was invited and better ways of fault reporting were discussed. They learned how to identify correctly which wheel sets were which and send fault reports to the depots to arrive before the train did. This last process was most beneficial to the service engineers who had the responsibility to carry out any repairs in optimum time.

The last day of the course they received their new uniforms and were invited to a farewell lunch with their InterCity manager. This was often Richard Brown, who at that time was InterCity manager for Midland Main Line. Richard was personable, the perfect gentleman. His appointment later to boss of Eurostar was one he truly deserved. Other regional 'celebrities' would arrive, often from InterCity marketing.

InterCity Midland Main Line marketing men often referred to the Bermuda Triangle. This was Derby, Leicester and Nottingham. It appeared that there was something out of 'kilter' with the thinking of the inhabitants of these three cities compared with the rest of the country. Market research discovered that when inhabitants were questioned as to what form of transport they would take to go any distance, they chose the bus ahead of the train. No one knew why they chose that, and it was put down to the considerable amount of railway closures during the 60s that had in some way made them think there were few trains left. Consequently, much effort had to be made by the marketing department to change their perception. Many within the 'Bermuda Triangle' were taken in by mass advertising, especially during primetime TV. They flocked to out-of-town discount furniture stores and DIY outlets at weekends after mass TV advertising, while many InterCity trains ran half empty between the Bermuda Triangle and other parts of the UK.

InterCity needed to create a larger market share of the travelling public. It wanted to capture more of the 'visiting friends and relations' market. This was a potentially huge market. If one could entice the weekend shopper to spend some of their money on travel instead of household luxuries then not only would it be good for InterCity but also good for the environment. After all, people were now becoming aware of the pollution caused by motorcars and the road building programmes. The Green Party was starting to make inroads and there was a lot of publicity from that quarter praising the benefit of rail travel.

InterCity went about attracting more passengers with a very grand and extremely successful ad campaign featuring the song So Relax by Leon Redbone. This became a huge hit and the advert worked. It also won many accolades and helped immensely the image of BR, especially InterCity, as a business. Excellent news of course for those pushing privatisation!

The success I had with LMST, Anglo-Danish and Senior Conductor Training for InterCity helped me make a further career move to the other side of the country. East Coast. I had enjoyed the cut and thrust of the LM and in particular the support and comrademanship of most of the senior managers, especially Cyril Bleasedale. He was known as Instant Cyril due to his quick decision-making when people asked him questions. These he would usually bounce back at you and would invite you to work on a project relating to your question. This ended up with one making a presentation of your findings in his office some weeks later. Consequently, people stopped asking him questions for fear of landing themselves with a project.

InterCity as a business was now starting to gear up for privatisation and the Conservative Government was hell bent on privatising anything they could, whatever the cost or detriment to the country. The great British public was being lambasted with adverts suggesting they buy shares in all the businesses with the prefix British: British Steel, British Gas, British Airways, British Telecom, B Sky B and very soon British Rail. We were to become a shareholder society.

If you consider the findings of 'Pareto' and the 80/20 principle, one can understand what a huge success this selling off of the family silver was to become. 80% of the public will go with the flow and feel left out if they don't, while the other 20%

who were less gullible were able to see through the media proper gander. Of course, if the 80/20 principle were reversed then there would be little advertising and possibly fewer wars, and certainly very few conscripts. The great British 'dumb-down' had started. One could easily apply the metaphor 'only dead fish follow the flow'. And this they did.

'Ask Sid' was a wonderful brainwashing ad for the sell-off of British Gas. Volunteers for both the Falklands and Iraq wars were another brainwash directed at the 80% and Maggie and the halfwit Reagan were well suited in creating a world of dumb-down folk. It worked, and we were to see the results of this many years on. Thankfully, most countries on the Continent saw Maggie and her privatisation scheme as suicidal. All that it would create would be a materialistic world where the UK would be just a service economy, manufacturing nothing, with European countries owning the lion's share of what had been traditionally British. Was this to be the plight of British Rail? By the late 80s the public were all in favour of the privatisation of British Rail. Little did they know what an utter disaster it would be. All they saw were the Government figures. The cost to the taxpayer. What they didn't realise was that privatisation would cost the taxpayer five times more than in the days of BR.

Safety would be eroded and fares increased to a level way above that of inflation

Not all of my time on the LM was wine and roses. There were some area managers who believed LMST had been a complete waste of time. These managers naturally caused their staff concern, and undermined the good work of those committed to the customer. These managers as well as being anti-customer service training also had a tendency to be anti-privatisation. They still saw the railways as a huge train set and they foolishly made their opinions and views known to the chairman Sir Bob Reid. He was not impressed with these renegades, and soon after, one morning, the news broke that all of them had been told to clear their desks. I, and many others rejoiced at this news, as these managers had contributed to the poor morale and poor service on BR. This was their just deserts.

CHAPTER 17

BRB HQ ER (York) and The Shadow Franchise

I was invited to attend an interview at the Eastern Regions HQ that was equivalent to the London Midland Regions BRB HQ. This was at the BRB HQ at York. The ER HQ was a wonderful turn-of-the-century building situated on Station Rise, York, and housed all the great and good responsible for everything railway on the Eastern side of Great Britain. The job offered was management development trainer for ICEC. (InterCity East Coast). ICEC was the shadow franchise set up as a forerunner to privatisation. ICEC was in its infancy. Privatisation was no longer just a rumour but fast becoming a reality.

I received confirmation of my post the same day as the interview and was immediately invited to attend the Christmas party at a pub on Blakey Ridge on the Yorkshire Moors. This invite came from the head of personnel, Mike McKechnie. Mike had been a graduate entree at St Pancras and I had first met him there, and subsequently at various wine tastings that were held underneath St Pancras station in the cellars that once housed the wines for all the British Transport Hotels. We both shared a passion for good food and wine, and it was thanks to Mike that ICEC became the leading on-train restaurant car service in Britain. Its trains became Michelin restaurants on wheels.

I arrived at York for the Christmas bash and joined the chartered bus with the East Coast personnel for the 'do' at The Lion on Blakey Ridge. I found myself sitting with two females with pronounced Yorkshire accents. I assumed wrongly that they were perhaps from the typing pool or admin. I was amazed to find that they were both senior ICEC managers. One was ICEC manager for Scotland! Learning point: do not assume that people with regional or local accents could not possibly hold a senior position. We played party games, got drunk, and had a good Christmas lunch. The coach had to stop many times on the way back to York as bladders became extended.

I started at York in the New Year, staying for the first six weeks at the Royal Station Hotel. This was a four-star hotel with one star service. It had been a superb hotel when BR had owned it, but along with all the other BR hotels had been sold off to a hotel chain only interested in creating shareholder value. Staff morale was low and the rooms needed refreshing. Inexperienced chefs produced industrial food that was served by reluctant, unsmiling staff in the dining room. My wife complaining that her steak was tough brought the response, "No problem, I'll bring you a sharper knife!" Breakfast brought yet another surprise when it was discovered one morning that the saltcellars had been filled with sugar, and that sugar bowls had been filled with salt! No doubt by some disgruntled member of staff.

I stayed at the Royal Station Hotel, as I was to be a delegate on a six-week course that would give me the qualifications to deliver ICEC's health and safety training programme to all staff that had safety-related posts. This task was in addition to the normal management training and development courses.

Four of us occupied the BRB training and development suite on Tanner Row, adjacent to the main HQ offices. It was Richard, Bob, Judy and myself. We got on famously from the word go and all suffered the same H&S course. We learnt just about everything to do with occupational health and hygiene and took several examinations that resulted in our NEBOSH (National Examination Board of Occupational Safety and Health) certificate.

My intention was to relocate to somewhere within striking distance of York: Thirsk, Northallerton or Malton, Malton being the favourite. That is, until I spent an evening there. What had appeared as a delightful market town during the day took on a menacing feel at night. Drunks and yobs took over the centre and made the town very unattractive. I decided that I would commute daily between Stamford and

York. I consequently abandoned the idea of living 'up north' again. After all, I had done that before, but on the other side of the Pennines. I soon learned to get into the Yorkshire style of humour. This was not too dissimilar to what I had been exposed to before on the west side of the Pennines.

BRB HQ at York was far more serious than the LM equivalent at Birmingham. This may have had something to do with the sombre interior of the building. It consisted of oak-lined corridors with heavy oak doors to every office. It was like something from the dark ages. It even had separate toilets for 'Officers' and 'Staff'! It would seem that any equal opportunities policies were unheard of in the corridors of power.

My immediate boss was Jim Dobson. If you could bottle what made Jim tick the world would be a much nicer place. He was supportive, human, extremely caring, had a wicked sense of humour and had the ability to be respected by all. He was the ideal HR (human resources) person. His job and personal specifications matched exactly. He also liked good food, real ale, malt whisky and good wine. He was a true epicurean. Jim enjoyed life, and we all liked being in Jim's company. With Mike McKechnie as head of personnel and Brian Burdsall as ICEC director, ICEC was formidable.

We commenced the health and safety courses with a three-day module for all managers and supervisors on East Coast. Workbooks consisting of 100 pages were produced along with videos and examination papers. All delegates had to pass an examination. This gave them the certificate necessary for British Rail to meet its safety case and comply with government legislation, most of which had been dreamed up in Brussels. We firmly believed that the Germans read it, the French laughed at it, and the English implemented it. But for us it was our bread and butter and we were now capable of boring for England with our newfound knowledge. We could clear a pub in 10 minutes flat.

These training courses were run at every main town along the line of route from Kings Cross to Glasgow and Edinburgh. Many of the delegates had to lodge in hotels during the course. The examination at the end of this event, which was compulsory for all those who attended, was not liked. Many railway personnel had not taken any form of exam since they left school. The questions were set by HQ safety advisors and were in sealed envelopes that were handed out by us, the trainers. We invigilated the exam and marked the papers.

The pass mark was set at 60%, but with room to negotiate on a one to one if absolutely necessary. Most staff passed without any problem. Those who failed took the exam and a one-day refresher course later. Imagine my surprise when one of my delegates turned out to be The Fonz! He failed. But only for a short while. I am too much of a humanist

to see him go back to his job with no certificate of competence. I had to conduct a question and answer session with him to ensure he had fully digested the content of the syllabus. He had. He was just one of several delegates who froze when confronted with an examination paper.

The Safety Programme was a huge success in so much that many employees were unaware of the potential dangers they were exposed to in their workplace. They did not notice the hazards within their workplace; they were blinkered to potential 'near misses'. The 'what if?' scenario. Thankfully, having visited workplace environments on other areas as part of a 'hazard hunt', they returned to their own place of work with a fresh pair of eyes.

It was hard to deliver the section on 'reporting of near misses' with conviction. After all, railway men had spent most of their working lives covering up for near misses. This new approach was perceived as 'snitching' and many of those attending would never report a near miss if one of their colleagues would be dropped in it. It took some convincing on the part of the trainer that we were now into a 'no blame' culture.

ICEC along with other shadow franchises had put in place a 'near miss, no blame' phone line. This would work well unless the same person kept leaving a message admitting to some misdemeanour. Would the person be identified? Of course he would. Would he be considered just a 'Jonah' or be considered a potential risk? And if so, should he be kept in his present post? Thankfully these decisions were not made by me, but by their immediate supervisor or manager.

The safety programme was just one of many new training programmes being introduced to conform to standards being set to comply with legislation brought about by the 'hidden' enquiry following Clapham, and the future privatisation of BR.

One management programme was entitled Coming to Agreement. This involved department heads attending a one-day seminar with trade union officials so that they fully understood their conditions of service and how things may or may not change under the new privatised ownership.

Each seminar had six heads of department and six trade union officials. Believe me, there was some heated debate and it was very difficult for the trainer to remain calm and impartial. Many trade unionists were steeped in the art of confrontation and had the ability to make a saint swear. The worst day was at Kings Cross when six ASLEF and RMT officials turned up and only two ICEC managers dared show their faces. It was the only time that I lost my temper while delivering a course. I dreaded reading the 'feedback appraisal form' completed by the delegates after the event, but strangely enough they were very complimentary about how I handled it all. I think they quite enjoyed the fire and brimstone approach.

Part of the course involved an exercise where we put both sides into conflict, and how they could then solve the problems that arose. This worked well and was followed by a session on understanding TUPE (Transfer of Undertakings and Protection of Employment Act). Without understanding how conflict can be caused and how it can be solved, TUPE would never have been accepted and the implementation of privatisation would have taken longer.

To develop and train staff was a main priority for ICEC and they set about delivering a Training and Development Road Show at all major cities between London and Edinburgh. These were held at leading city centre hotels and offered any member of staff a chance to chat with those responsible for training and development and discuss their training needs. Of course, this process existed for senior management through their annual performance review, but for those beneath the management scale there was little chance for this to happen.

The HQ trainers discovered that there was a huge wealth of talent in the lower ranks that managers had not been aware of. People with degrees working as a railman, a young Olympic gold medallist working in a booking office, and a round-the-world sailor in a telephone enquiry bureau. If people had this amount of ability then surely we should be developing that person so as to benefit themselves and the business.

We all like some challenge in our lives. However, it is no good offering someone a career if all they want is a job. Likewise, it is no good giving someone just a job if it is a career they crave. The railways had always been good at addressing the latter. Now, thanks to the foresight of Mike McKechnie and Jim Dobson, who championed this initiative, all this trapped talent was to be released. Yet it was the new order of privatisation that would benefit from the last endeavours of BR.

Meanwhile, back in Mudeford Plum was getting difficult. Evening trips from York down to Christchurch, and worse still to Bournemouth hospital to see Plum were becoming less appreciated and difficult. Plum would have done well to have a season ticket for Bournemouth Hospital as she was one of their best customers. She was either discovering a new complaint, wishing she had one, or planning to have one.

Many of her problems latterly stemmed from her patent cure for constipation, which involved sitting on a bucket of hot steam to induce movement. This resulted in third degree burns. Skin grafts followed, as did infection after her dog was allowed to share her bed.

I am a firm believer that when one gets to 80 years of age, the children become the parents of the parents. This was certainly the case where Plum was concerned.

She had now become very bitter, falling out with all her friends and neighbours. Many of these people had been very good to her but one by one they fell by the wayside. She threatened to die on our holiday in order that she might spoil any pleasure we might have that she was not privileged to. And yes, she did die on our holiday. In fact, we had just arrived at Appleby Manor Hotel in Cumbria when the manager announced the news to me about Plum. We arranged a funeral with an undertaker in Bournemouth from our hotel room and decided that there was little else to be done.

It had started to snow in Appleby and we walked to the railway station deep in conversation about Plum and her demise. My sombre mood was changed once I saw steam from Coronation pacific *Duchess of Hamilton* arrive with an enthusiasts' special. It stopped, set back and did a photographic run past. This was a wonderful send-off for Plum! However, the actual send-off for Plum was a grim affair. This took place in the elephants' graveyard – Bournemouth Crematorium. It involved the hearse and mourners queuing up waiting for their slot, a situation akin to an airport take-off procedure. Eventually we were allowed in and the ceremony started. The vicar was wonderfully confused, possibly due to both he and I being under the influence of alcohol when I briefed him about Plum's life. He read out the wrong details pertaining to Plum's time on earth, referring to her as a nurse! However, he did get the audio aspect right. The Sound of Music. This was Plum's favourite piece of music and she had seen the film 25 times.

I requested the taxi immediately after the ceremony to make haste to Bournemouth Central so I could return quickly away from this morbid place. The train home made sweet music and rapid progress north. The grim surroundings of Birmingham New Street being slightly better than Bournemouth Crematorium. It was some time later at Bournemouth's hospital, while collecting Plum's personal belongings, that I discovered she had not died when we thought but some time after. Evidently the hospital had mixed Plum up with another women in the same ward. And although Plum had wanted her body to go to medical science, the final blow came when this was refused. The reason given was that there were already too many Plums.

CHAPTER 18

Severance!

New '12-year-old' graduate managers were arriving off the production line along with 'look at me, aren't I gorgeous?' bimbos, who had no experience in the railway culture or business, and even less in man management skills. The old order were being offered 'severance packages' and those staff with the most experience and ability were clamouring for early retirement. Any 'old farts' above 50 were considered unsuitable for this new regime. Pay rewards for leaving the service were generous, and the dangled carrot attracted many senior managers.

By now privatisation was becoming a reality and Prime Minister John Major was hell-bent in seeing it through before his inevitable fall from power, thus leaving the mess to the next incoming government.

Railway people were scared. Vacancies appeared in the new businesses. The new businesses and the vacancies on offer were alien to many of the staff. The duplication of posts! It looked like there was to be more staff than at present. And there was. People would be allocated to one of the businesses and many of the old traditional posts that would have had only one supervisor or manager covering

Potters Bar. An accident as a result of privatisation. Checks and balances were lacking with the P-way contractors and subcontractors.

all the function, were now to have several; one for each business! Firstly, one had to be identified with a business. InterCity was the favourite, while Regional Railways was considered second division, and Railfreight was considered bottom of the league. Therefore, ICEC attracted the cream.

The engineering and telecom functions were being taken over by any new start-up business. I lost count of how many different businesses there would be when it passed the 100 mark. Another 'Clapham' was inevitable. Profit was what it was all about, with financial gurus taking charge. Experienced railway men were deserting the sinking ship, frustrated at seeing all the disasters unfolding before their eyes.

Worst of all was the lack of checks and balances within the permanent way departments. Contractors and sub contractors with little railway experience were employed through newly set up employment agencies. Certificates issued for working on a railway line were changing hands on the black market and agency workers often swapped their weekend duties with a friend, handing over their certificate in the process. No checks at the worksite existed. We didn't have to wait long for the disasters to happen – Potters Bar and Hatfield followed in fairly quick succession, and then Paddington.

New systems were being introduced. The worst perhaps being 'fast-track' driver training. It had now become possible for a new recruit to start a driver training course in the early spring and be qualified by late November, having never experienced fog, or stopping a train on icy leaves.

Ken Loach's film The Navigators says it all, and this was made before many of the disasters happened.

Jim Dobson our stupendous boss put his hand up for the golden handshake, as did Richard, Judy, Bob and myself. Mike McKechnie gave us the Papal blessing and at 48 years of age I took early retirement.

It had been suggested that we went down the management buyout route and took over the Boards Training Division, which with hindsight would have made us a fortune, but Bob and I had other ideas.

I did not want to dip into my severance pay. I still had two years to wait before I could draw my railway pension at the age of 50. Bob was two years younger than me and had heavy family commitments. He needed an income. But as we left the employ of ICEC on the Friday we started a consultancy business on the following Monday. Our first contract was for a development-training programme for all Bounds Green InterCity Depot staff. This involved a series of five-day outward-bound type courses linked to workplace activities. Word had got around that Bob and myself had started our own business. We already had a good reputation, and considering that most of the railway experience had been thrown out with the 'bathwater', the new railway managers were eager to employ us. We received a government start-up grant and called our training and development business Train 2000.

Our redundancy or severance pay was invested and we were given advice by a financial advisor, consequently investing our golden handshake with several FTSE companies. Our financial advisor would have been better employed as a bus conductor and it was some years later that I managed to turn round the loss incurred by his so-called secure investments.

Train 2000 was soon going from strength to strength with much work coming in from the new privatised railway companies. They were desperately seeking specialised training and development. New laws now meant that we had to tender for work, which often led Train 2000 to compete with some pretty major training establishments, but every time we won the tender. This must really have pissed off some of the 'big boys', but they were not up to speed with the systems of railway, its culture, and had little of the management skill required to deliver what was needed in this new railway world.

Bob and I worked hard to acquire more and more clients and during the second year of trading we were awarded a commendation for our work towards health and safety. Everyone's favourite business guru Sir John Harvey Jones presented this award.

We were now delivering safety training for what had become GNER (Great North Eastern Railway), now led by its new boss Christopher Garnett. Although the Government had probably instigated his appointment, he seemed to have the right ideas for running the East Coast Main Line. He certainly appeared more capable than the politicians who appointed him. With James Sherwood, president of the American company Sea Containers backing him, there was not a lot that could go wrong. After all, Mike McKechnie had put in place the benchmarks while the Sherwood emporium only needed to follow on with some of their own ideas brought about by the experience they had gleaned from their Orient Express ownership. This all gave GNER the publicity and kudos necessary. It fast became the privatised railway flagship all the others aspired to.

Mike McKechnie left the sinking ship and joined the board of Granada while many of the senior managers went wandering off to pastures new. I firmly believe that neither Bob nor I realised how much in demand railway managers were by major UK businesses. The training given to management by BR was considered some of the best in the country and it wasn't long before major PLCs were asking us to deliver bespoke training for their organisation. This of course was excellent news, but very stressful.

Most of the training we delivered was residential and therefore many hotels and conference

Hatfield. Another privatisation result.

centres were chasing us to run events at their establishments. We listened to what they offered, made further demands, and accepted a free weekend break just to put them under the microscope. We now had an admirable portfolio that consisted of about 50% railway safety training, 30% management development for senior railway bosses, and 20% for FTSE 100 companies. The latter being mainly banks, insurance, and distribution organisations. Others included those in the SME sectors (small and medium sized enterprises). These consisted of hotel and restaurant chains, manufacturing, building and service industries. We especially enjoyed working with the Relais and Chateaux Hotels and Restaurants. Their excellent customer service, food and wine would have been ample substitute for any fee! Our client base was now impressive with many 'top drawer' businesses.

This period in my life left little time for social activities. I had little interest in the music world,

concentrated on personnel consultancy, recruitment and employment law, along with designing and installing tailor-made computer systems for the retail and distribution trade. Our roles often crossed and we found ourselves then working for the same enterprise. Many were located along the M62 corridor and we were able to monitor the progress of GNER and other TOCs (Train Operating Companies).

In consultancy terms the railway businesses were difficult to shake off, and hardly a week went by without one of the TOCs requesting some advice or training. Again, the portfolio was diverse, although there was no intention to deliver training to the extent I had in Train 2000 days.

However, I did find myself back on the rail industry treadmill. By now I was working freelance for some of the UK's leading management consultants, and through them, found myself designing, delivering and facilitating management development programmes for Great Western, Northern Spirit, and Railtrack. Along with the SME sector the workload was again getting out of hand.

The rail industry was in 'panic mode'. Many of the newly appointed managers arrived through default as recruitment policies were inadequate. Anyone with railway management experience could demand astronomical fees, and did. This appalling situation the railways found themselves in sadly helped create charlatan consultants, many of who did more harm than good. It was a case of the blind leading the blind. It caused great frustration for the few existing employees who hadn't had the opportunity to leave the sinking ship before the new regime. Morale was low, motivation non-existent and the future insecure. In spite of TUPE (Transfer of Undertakings Protection of Employment Act) employees were becoming more and more concerned about their long-term prospects, as TUPE only appeared to guarantee the same working conditions for the first transfer. Franchises were changing as often as football managers.

This situation was a godsend for the trade union movement, and both ASLEF and the RMT lost little time in flexing their muscles. Meanwhile, the Conservative government ministers responsible for rail privatisation had now handed over the reins to Labour who would consequently be blamed for all the problems.

I recall spending an especially difficult week with senior executives of Railtrack developing action plans for their business. Each day new problems arose and it was felt that by the end of the week nothing would be achieved. However, as often happened, everything fell into place on the last day and both my associate and I went home satisfied. The following week, however, most of those senior executives were moved out of their offices and subsequently nothing came of the action-planning week! This was the start of Railtrack's demise.

and absolutely no interest in Wet Wet Wet, Boyzone or Bros – all of them being 'designer groups' with far more publicity and marketing than talent. Work took up 18 hours a day, seven days a week. I could bore for England! Overweight, run down and stressed with work pressure I decided to quit the successful Train 2000 partnership and hand it over to Bob.

I formed a less demanding enterprise with my wife and concentrated on non-executive directorships, management buy-outs and joint ventures. My wife

It is very frustrating being invited to turn around the thinking of some organisations only to find that the chairman or chief executive, after initiating a development programme for their executives, has suddenly had a change of heart and altered many of the initiatives brought about by their senior execs. All too often, CEOs felt that any form of development was beneath them, when in actual fact they were in need of it the most.

Often family businesses faltered because the third-generation halfwit son had inherited the role of chief executive. Real talent within an organisation often went unnoticed, and many businesses lost out through nepotism. Nonetheless we were in a prime position to spot talent. A fresh pair of eyes overlooking a business and its employees will notice far more than those in command. Many senior managers were often too close to the problems to recognise any shortfall within their organisation. The person who creates a problem seldom manages to solve it. The newly privatised rail businesses were a prime example.

I enjoyed my journeys by train to all the many different commissions, and in particular, the excellent restaurant car meals and service offered on GNER. Privatisation had become patchy. GNER was excellent, and to a lesser degree so were Midland Mainline, Anglia and Chiltern. These were all shaping up, but there were some pretty poor attempts at delivering the goods by other TOCs. Many had lost direction. Virgin recruited many ex-railway managers to try and knock it all together and successfully persuaded Chris Green to bring some semblance of order back to West Coast. His excellent managerial style helped motivate a demotivated workforce.

Chris was liked and respected by all the rail industry. He was irreplaceable, while Great Western just went from bad to worse. This was down to poor appointments at the top and an inferior recruitment policy. After all, bus companies didn't have the ability and management skills to run railways. Shareholder value and greed that were the key objectives. Service to the public did not enter into it.

There were several TOCs likely to lose their government franchise. In fact, some did. During the transition period, newly appointed managers with little railway experience clamoured for help and advice, and it was nice to be in demand and be able to try and do some good.

Much of what took place under privatisation would have happened anyway under BR. All privatisation achieved was a change in the colour of the train sets, demoralisation of the workforce and a cost to the great British taxpayer that was five times greater than in the halcyon days of BR. But at least the shareholders profited by it.

I had the pleasure and misfortune of training many of the new breed of managers early on in their careers while at BRB HQ, York, and I am not surprised

that the newly privatised railways in the UK became the laughing stock of Europe. At one time a railway manager could have commanded a senior position in any organisation; I fear that this would not be the case with this new wave of managers. Educational standards in schools and universities have seriously gone astray. Good degree results had become easier thanks to lowering of benchmarks and personal development has become virtually non-existent. This new breed totally lacking basic interpersonal skills. Many graduates being no further advanced in business terms after their three years at university than school leavers.

Psychometric tests of dubious sources were springing up in every HR department and being applied as the main tool for recruitment. Many unsuitable individuals were getting recruited into quite senior positions through this process. Gone were the days of tried and tested recruitment methods.

EMAP plc believed in a 'grow your own' policy with a continuous development programme for all its employees. This worked. BR had a similar policy in its halcyon days, which also worked. But now it is all down to short-term management positions hell-bent on change. Any fool can change something; few nowadays stay in their role long enough to see the errors of their ways. Similar to government ministers!

Work overload again became a problem. I started to refuse some of the more stressful work and concentrated on winning back some of my severance pay that the 'wonderful' financial advisor had lost me. I studied the AIM (Alternative Investment Market). I read all I could, planned and designed an imaginary investment portfolio and watched its performance over a year.

I became pleasantly surprised and decided to go 'live' and take a chance for real. I spent hours watching the computer screen when I was without a commission, and after a few months managed to claw back what had been lost. I soon found out that I could make more by staying at home than going out to work. So that was what I did. I had spent too much time earning money and not enough time making money. Was I becoming obsessed with wealth and greed? Was I doing what Maggie, all those years ago, had wanted us to do? Was I becoming too stressed? Of course I was and at the age of 53 I suffered a heart attack.

I was taken by ambulance with little petrol in its tank to Peterborough hospital, dropped from the stretcher onto the floor, and left in a corridor where workmen were rebuilding the hospital around the patients. After some time, a young lady doctor dressed in RAF uniform arrived and examined me, attaching me to a heart monitor. That was that. An hour later I was told to go home and make an appointment with my GP. This I did. My GP had heard nothing from Peterborough and just told me to watch my diet and take things easy.

I now believe that the term general practitioner means just that. GPs seem reluctant to refer you to specialists, preferring to diagnose your problem themselves. Doctors' practice managers did everything within their power to stop you seeing the doctor, or worse still tried to diagnose any problem themselves! Nurses appeared at what was called a 'well man's clinic' where a cursory glance enabled them to say you were A1. The examination involved taking blood pressure, blowing down a tube, and peeing in a bottle. And that was that. Results were seldom discussed and unless there was something really obvious then nothing more would be heard. Certainly nothing proactive took place. The NHS had become a huge administration vehicle, overseeing cost-cutting of the services that were the very reason for its existence.

It was Neil Kinnock who once said: "You had better not become old or ill under a Tory government." How right he was, although few believed it at the time as we were all clamouring for this materialistic world of greed and avarice. We were all buying shares,

bigger houses and cars to impress our neighbours, most of this being on credit. If only hindsight was foresight. But now Tony had arrived and inherited the problems that had been brought about by the previous governments. Would he recreate BR? He did seem to have the right ideas, but sadly the wrong priorities. He preferred to get involved in wars.

Many years later, he got blamed for all the ills of the country that Maggie and Major had created. Hey ho, such is politics. For some time we had considered moving from England to somewhere different. The heart attack event had pulled me up sharp. It was the gypsy's warning. I began to think less about the materialistic and money grabbing world of Maggie's disciples and more about Tom and Barbara in the Good Life. I desperately wanted to change my life. I felt sullied. The fetid breath of capitalism was becoming more and more acrid. I wanted to grow old in a caring society, with an excellent health service, the sun on my back and a glass in my hand. I decided enough was enough, retired, and started a new life in France.

The Author

From an early life in pursuit of steam trains in the East Midlands to the world of drugs, rock and roll and the music business in London. The author has tried to capture the changing scene of the rail industry from steam to privatisation, and the music industry from ballad through pop to rock, all from personal involvement.

Privately educated in a second-rate public school in Nottingham and rejecting the silver spoon of the family business, Richard chose a route encompassing both music and railways – though he was never too sure which he preferred. This took him through the halcyon years of the 60s and 70s heavy rock music period and the catastrophic privatisation years of Thatcher. In both camps Richard took a lead role and this is his tale. Richard lives in Lozere France with his wife Janet and cat. He is recognised as an authority on rail matters and contributes to magazines in both the UK and France. He continues to play in an Anglo-French rhythm & blues band.

The author today.

Appendix One

Nucleus Entertainments, Wardour Street W1

The Temple Club on Wardour Street had originally been the Flamingo Club which was a jazz venue formed by Jeff Kruger who was a pop entrepreneur. Jeff, along with Hal Shaper (a record plugger), helped form Sparta Florida Music and Beacon Records.

Andrew Loog Oldham (the Rolling Stones' first manager) had been barman at the Flamingo and became involved with what is now known as the Jeff Kruger Organisation. This organisation later obtained the music publishing rights to many of the leading recording artistes of the day, including Frank Sinatra, Glen Campbell and later many of the rock bands of the 70s.

The Temple Club became the vehicle for all new aspiring progressive rock bands to become recognised.

Nucleus was the agency that handled the bookings and the artistes for the Temple Club. Stu Dingley, along with Ron Hire*, Neil Thompson and myself were all involved in handling the acts signed to the agency and for booking all the acts in the Temple Club.

These were; Blonde on Blonde, Warhorse, UFO, Shaking Stevens and the Sunsets, Pete Brown's Piblokto, Flying Hat Band, Radha Krishna Temple and Budgie.

Acorn Artistes, Dean Street, London W1

Those employed at Acorn Artistes to handle agency and management of many of the pop groups of the 70s were; Col Johnson, John Salter, Chris Morrison, Brian Longley, Keith Rossiter, Steve Elson, Mike Rispoli, Colin Thurling and myself.

The Acts associated with Acorn Artistes were Marmalade, Middle of the Road, The Equals, Christie, Eddison Lighthouse, Love Affair, DBM and The Foundations, Johnny Johnson and the Bandwagon, Fairweather, Thin Lizzy, Status Quo, Danta, Worth, Picketywitch, Arrival, New Seekers, Barabus and Nimbus.

DCA, London WC2

Pretty Things, Jon Darnborough Band, T2, *The Flying Hat Band and Slowbone.

---

*Ron Hire managed Warhorse led by Nick Simper, bass guitarist with Deep Purple. Ron, along with Messrs. Phil Edwards and John Coletta, formed a management company – HEC Enterprises.

*Discovered by World Wide Artistes Ian Anderson and Patrick Mehan.

Appendix Two

1969-1972 groups appearing at the Temple Club, booked by Nucleus were as follows:

Genesis, Slade, Pretty Things, Super Tramp, Fleetwood Mac, Comus, Pete Brown and Piblokto, May Blitz, Noir, Edgar Broughton, Taste, Stray, Brian Auger, Curved Air, Beggars Opera, Mungo Jerry, Patto, Steamhammer, Hackensack, Flying Fortress, Van der Graf Generator, Audience, Wishbone Ash, Procal Harum, Gnome Sweet Gnome, Paul-Brett Sage, Ralph McTell, Hawkwind, Barclay James Harvest, Cochise, Robert Kray, Mighty Baby, Roy Young Band, Warm Dust, Groundhogs, Status Quo, Jackson Brown, Uriah Heap, Sasafras, Nazareth, Danta, Budgie, Gravy Train, T2, Brinsley Swartz, Renaissance, Pink Fairies, Sam Apple Pie, UFO, Blodwyn Pig, Phillip Goodhand Tate, Writing on the Wall, Warhorse, Shaking Stevens, Sunshine, Badfinger, Arthur Brown, Quicksilver, Quatermass, Heads Hands and Feet, Blonde on Blonde, Smile, who later became Queen.

Appendix Three

Signal Boxes worked

Toton Centre (box lad), Castle Donington, Long Eaton, Kimberley, Hasland Sidings, Clay Cross North Junction, Northolt Junction East, Kensington South Main, Buxton No.1, Hindlow, Dove Holes, Chapel-en-les-Frith South, Whaley Bridge, Furness Vale, Disley, Norbury Crossing, Hazel Grove NW, Woodsmoor, Edgeley Junction No.1, Hazel Grove Midland, New Mills South Junction, Chinley Station North Junction, Chinley North Junction, Peak Forest South, Great Rocks Junction, Edale, Earls Sidings, Bamford, Grindleford, Carlton, Bingham, Wyfordby Crossing, Melton Mowbray, Wymondham Crossing, Saxby Juntion, Whissendine, Oakham Level Crossing, Manton Junction, Langham Junction and Luffenham Junction.